Macmillan/McGraw-Hill Science

OCEANS OF AIR

AUTHORS

Mary Atwater
The University of Georgia

Prentice Baptiste
University of Houston

Lucy Daniel
Rutherford County Schools

Jay Hackett
University of Northern Colorado

Richard Moyer
University of Michigan, Dearborn

Carol Takemoto
Los Angeles Unified School District

Nancy Wilson
Sacramento Unified School District

Inland Passage, Alaska

Macmillan/McGraw-Hill School Publishing Company
New York   Chicago   Columbus

MACMILLAN / McGRAW-HILL

SCIENCE TURNS MINDS ON ™

CONSULTANTS

Assessment:

Janice M. Camplin
Curriculum Coordinator, Elementary Science
Mentor, Western New York
Lake Shore Central Schools
Angola, NY

Mary Hamm
Associate Professor
Department of Elementary Education
San Francisco State University
San Francisco, CA

Cognitive Development:

Dr. Elisabeth Charron
Assistant Professor of Science Education
Montana State University
Bozeman, MT

Sue Teele
Director of Education Extension
University of California, Riverside
Riverside, CA

Cooperative Learning:

Harold Pratt
Executive Director of Curriculum
Jefferson County Public Schools
Golden, CO

Earth Science:

Thomas A. Davies
Research Scientist
The University of Texas
Austin, TX

David G. Futch
Associate Professor of Biology
San Diego State University
San Diego, CA

Dr. Shadia Rifai Habbal
Harvard-Smithsonian Center for Astrophysics
Cambridge, MA

Tom Murphree, Ph.D.
Global Systems Studies
Monterey, CA

Suzanne O'Connell
Assistant Professor
Wesleyan University
Middletown, CT

Environmental Education:

Cheryl Charles, Ph.D.
Executive Director
Project Wild
Boulder, CO

Gifted:

Sandra N. Kaplan
Associate Director, National/State Leadership
Training Institute on the Gifted/Talented
Ventura County Superintendent of Schools Office
Northridge, CA

Global Education:

M. Eugene Gilliom
Professor of Social Studies and Global Education
The Ohio State University
Columbus, OH

Merry M. Merryfield
Assistant Professor of Social Studies and Global Education
The Ohio State University
Columbus, OH

Intermediate Specialist

Sharon L. Strating
Missouri State Teacher of the Year
Northwest Missouri State University
Marysville, MO

Life Science:

Carl D. Barrentine
Associate Professor of Biology
California State University
Bakersfield, CA

V.L. Holland
Professor and Chair, Biological Sciences Department
California Polytechnic State University
San Luis Obispo, CA

Donald C. Lisowy
Education Specialist
New York, NY

Dan B. Walker
Associate Dean for Science Education and Professor of Biology
San Jose State University
San Jose, CA

Literature:

Dr. Donna E. Norton
Texas A&M University
College Station, TX

Tina Thoburn, Ed.D.
President
Thoburn Educational Enterprises, Inc.
Ligonier, PA

Macmillan/McGraw-Hill School Division
10 Union Square East
New York, New York 10003

Printed in the United States of America

ISBN 0-02-274269-7 / 4

5 6 7 8 9 VHJ 99 98 97 96 95 94 93

Cumulus clouds

Mathematics:

Martin L. Johnson
Professor, Mathematics Education
University of Maryland at College Park
College Park, MD

Physical Science:

Max Diem, Ph.D.
Professor of Chemistry
City University of New York, Hunter College
New York, NY

Gretchen M. Gillis
Geologist
Maxus Exploration Company
Dallas, TX

Wendell H. Potter
Associate Professor of Physics
Department of Physics
University of California, Davis
Davis, CA

Claudia K. Viehland
Educational Consultant, Chemist
Sigma Chemical Company
St. Louis, MO

Reading:

Jean Wallace Gillet
Reading Teacher
Charlottesville Public Schools
Charlottesville, VA

Charles Temple, Ph. D.
Associate Professor of Education
Hobart and William Smith Colleges
Geneva, NY

Safety:

Janice Sutkus
Program Manager: Education
National Safety Council
Chicago, IL

Science Technology and Society (STS):

William C. Kyle, Jr.
Director, School Mathematics and Science Center
Purdue University
West Lafayette, IN

Social Studies:

Mary A. McFarland
Instructional Coordinator of
Social Studies, K-12, and
Director of Staff Development
Parkway School District
St. Louis, MO

Students Acquiring English:

Mrs. Bronwyn G. Frederick, M.A.
Bilingual Teacher
Pomona Unified School District
Pomona, CA

Misconceptions:

Dr. Charles W. Anderson
Michigan State University
East Lansing, MI

Dr. Edward L. Smith
Michigan State University
East Lansing, MI

Multicultural:

Bernard L. Charles
Senior Vice President
Quality Education for Minorities Network
Washington, DC

Cheryl Willis Hudson
Graphic Designer and Publishing Consultant
Part Owner and Publisher, Just Us Books, Inc.
Orange, NJ

Paul B. Janeczko
Poet
Hebron, MA

James R. Murphy
Math Teacher
La Guardia High School
New York, NY

Ramon L. Santiago
Professor of Education and Director of ESL
Lehman College, City University of New York
Bronx, NY

Clifford E. Trafzer
Professor and Chair, Ethnic Studies
University of California, Riverside
Riverside, CA

STUDENT ACTIVITY TESTERS

Jennifer Kildow
Brooke Straub
Cassie Zistl
Betsy McKeown
Seth McLaughlin
Max Berry
Wayne Henderson

FIELD TEST TEACHERS

Sharon Ervin
San Pablo Elementary School
Jacksonville, FL

Michelle Gallaway
Indianapolis Public School #44
Indianapolis, IN

Kathryn Gallman
#7 School
Rochester, NY

Karla McBride
#44 School
Rochester, NY

Diane Pease
Leopold Elementary
Madison, WI

Kathy Perez
Martin Luther King Elementary
Jacksonville, FL

Ralph Stamler
Thoreau School
Madison, WI

Joanne Stern
Hilltop Elementary School
Glen Burnie, MD

Janet Young
Indianapolis Public School #90
Indianapolis, IN

CONTRIBUTING WRITER

Jim Gorman

OCEANS OF AIR

Lessons   **Themes**

Unit Introduction **Oceans of Air** ..... Systems and Interactions **6**
Did you know that a cricket can tell you the temperature?

1 **Getting in Touch With Air** .... Systems and Interactions **12**
Inside, outside, and all around, air is everywhere.

2 **Why Does the Wind Blow?** .... Systems and Interactions **24**
How can you tell which way the wind is blowing? What makes it change? What causes the wind to blow in the first place?

3 **How Does a Cloud Form?** .... Energy **34**
What do the mirror in your bathroom and a cloud have in common?

4 **Why Does the Weather Change?** ... Patterns of Change **46**
How does a storm turn into a tornado? You don't have to be Dorothy to find out.

5 **Weather, Climate, and You** .... Systems and Interactions **62**
Everybody talks about the weather. What do you do about it?

Unit Wrap Up **Understanding Air, Weather, and Climate** .... Systems and Interactions **72**
Rain. Snow. Hot. Cold. Around the world you have your choice of weather and climate.

Activities!

EXPLORE

Making Magic With Air 14

Can You Measure Wind Speed? 26

What Makes a Cloud? 36

Getting in Front of Weather Changes 48

Discovering Climate in North America 64

TRY THIS

Massive Amounts of Air 17

Air Power 18

Warming Up Fast or Slow 29

The Sun and Evaporation 39

Cooling Off 41

Cloud Watching 43

Move Aside, Here I Come! 51

Forecasting the Weather 59

Polar Zebra 69

As the World Turns 74

Features

Links

Literature Link
Science in Literature **10**

Weather **53**

Hurricane! **57**

Health Link
Nature's Air Conditioner **41**

Blocking Out the Sun **71**

Social Studies Link
Let Us Plant Lettuce! **67**

Worldwide Weather Disasters **72**

GLOBAL VIEW
Stormy Weather Worldwide **60**

CAREERS
Blimp Pilot **16**

SCIENCE TECHNOLOGY AND Society

Focus on Technology
Sailing for One **31**

Wind Energy for the Future **32**

Focus on Environment
Rain Shadow **44**

Making Deserts Green? **45**

Departments
Glossary **76**

Index **78**

Credits **80**

Oceans of Air

Think about the people who lived hundreds of years ago. What did they know about the weather? How did they learn about storms? What if you had lived many years ago and had no one to explain the weather to you? What would you think about thunder? What would you do if you were outdoors in a snowstorm? Would knowing about weather be important to you?

Minds On! There are lots of ways to describe snow—wet snow, falling snow, soft snow, snow crystals, and drifting snow, for example. Close your eyes and think of rain. How would you describe it? What would you call a gentle rain, or a spring rain, or a heavy rain? With a partner, think of five different ways to describe rain. Make up a word for each description. Share your rain vocabulary with your class. ●

An Inuit looks out over the frozen landscape near the Arctic Circle.

Long ago, people learned about storms by watching the skies for signs. Clouds, wind, and the way animals behaved before a storm helped teach people to prepare for bad weather.

When the wind changes direction, a sailor knows that a storm is not far away.

When birds gather on telephone wires, it is usually a sign that rain is coming. Low air pressure makes it difficult for birds to fly.

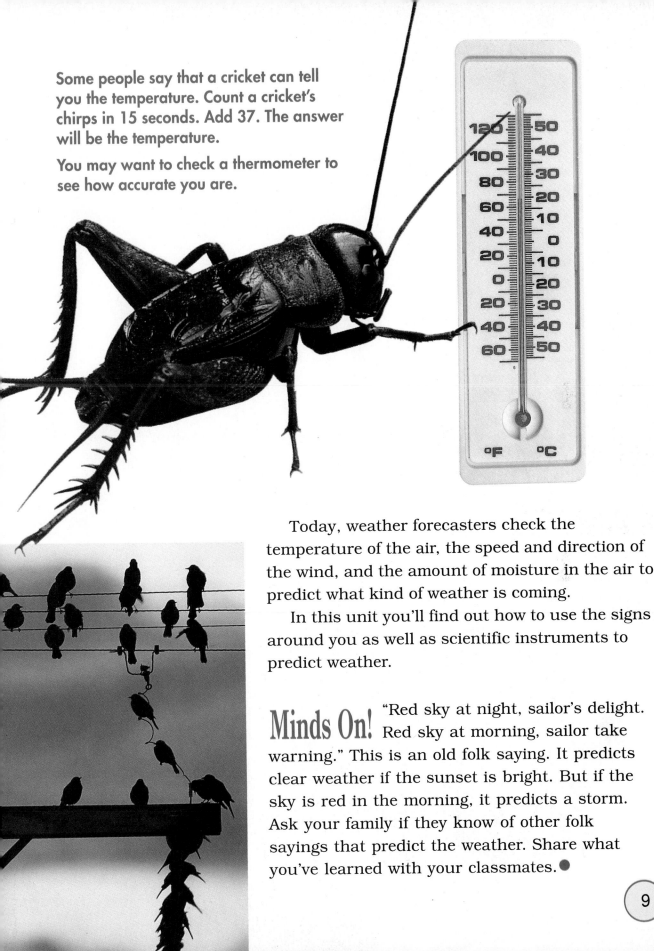

Some people say that a cricket can tell you the temperature. Count a cricket's chirps in 15 seconds. Add 37. The answer will be the temperature.

You may want to check a thermometer to see how accurate you are.

Today, weather forecasters check the temperature of the air, the speed and direction of the wind, and the amount of moisture in the air to predict what kind of weather is coming.

In this unit you'll find out how to use the signs around you as well as scientific instruments to predict weather.

Minds On! "Red sky at night, sailor's delight. Red sky at morning, sailor take warning." This is an old folk saying. It predicts clear weather if the sunset is bright. But if the sky is red in the morning, it predicts a storm. Ask your family if they know of other folk sayings that predict the weather. Share what you've learned with your classmates. ●

Science in Literature

People have always been curious about the weather, especially storms. Does watching a storm of any kind make you shiver with excitement? Reading about weather and storms can be just as interesting as watching them. Here are some fascinating books about storms, hurricanes, and tornadoes that you might enjoy reading.

Hurricane!
by Faith McNulty.
New York: Harper and Row, 1983.

John helps his parents prepare for a New England hurricane. He learns to observe weather signs from animals, birds, and the sky. These signs tell him that a big storm is coming. John observes from the safety of his home but worries about his tree house in the big, old tree outside his back door. Will they both outlast the storm? Look for signs of the approaching hurricane as you read this book.

Weather
by Howard E. Smith, Jr.
New York: Doubleday, 1990.

Everything you have ever wanted to know about weather is in this book. You can read about blizzards, dust storms, hurricanes, and tornadoes. You'll be amazed when you read about the problems that happen when fog and pollution combine. If you are concerned about Earth's future, you'll be interested in reading about future climates.

Other Good Books To Read

The Science Book of Air
by Neil Ardley.
New York: Harcourt Brace Jovanovich, 1991.

This book has wonderful experiments that are easy and fun to do. Discover all the properties of air for yourself and amaze your friends, too!

Tornado Alert
by Franklin M. Branley.
New York: Thomas Y. Crowell, 1988.

What is a tornado? How do you know a tornado is coming? How dangerous can this storm be? Would you know how to protect yourself if you heard a tornado warning? Read this book to find out more about the funnel-shaped storm we call a tornado.

The Mystery of the Double Double
Cross by Mary Blount Christian.
Niles, IL: Albert Whitman and Company, 1982.

Jeff gets kidnapped by mistake and finds himself in the middle of a terrible hurricane. Read this book to find out more about Jeff's adventure. How does he survive the hurricane and his kidnappers?

Storms by Seymour Simon.
New York: Morrow Junior Books, 1989.

Did you know that there are about 16 million thunderstorms around the world each year? If you want to read about thunderstorms, tornadoes, and hurricanes, this book is for you!

Getting in Touch With

Do you like riddles? Try this one. What has no color, no taste, and no smell but can sometimes knock you off your feet? Discover the answer in this lesson.

People and animals need air because their bodies need oxygen and other gases to live. You could live without food or water for several days, but you would live only minutes without air.

Air is invisible, but you can see that it takes up space when a balloon expands as you blow it up. You can see air rippling the grass and whipping the oceans into white-capped waves. You can't smell air, but odors of every kind reach your nose by currents of air.

Air is made up of about one-fifth oxygen and four-fifths nitrogen.

There are also small amounts of other gases, including water vapor and carbon dioxide. Air allows plants and animals to exchange the oxygen and carbon dioxide that living things need to survive.

Air can work for us in other ways, too. The jackhammer that breaks up concrete and a dentist's drill are powered by air. Air bags are used in cars to protect drivers and passengers.

Minds On! In your *Activity Log* on page 1, write two ways you can prove that air is around you. Compare your ideas with those of a classmate. ●

Having fun with a giant
soap bubble

Activity!

Making Magic With Air

You and your classmates could come up with a long list of evidence proving that air is everywhere. The following activities will offer even more evidence.

What You Need

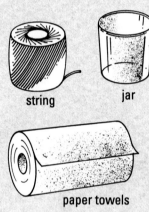

string   jar

Activity Log pages 2-3

water

2 balloons

straight pin

paper towels

plastic shoe box

cardboard

metric ruler

scissors

What To Do

Part A

1 Fill the plastic box half full of water.

2 Crumble a paper towel and place it in the jar.

3 Predict what will happen when the jar is put upside down in the water.

4 Hold the jar with the open end down and push it straight down to the bottom of the plastic box without tilting it. Record your observations.

Safety!

See the *Safety Tip* in step 3 of Part C.

Part B

1 Cut a square from the cardboard larger than the diameter of the plastic jar.

2 Fill the jar half full of water. Place the cut section of the cardboard over the mouth of the jar.

3 Predict what will happen when the jar is turned upside down.

4 Flip the jar over as you hold the cardboard in place. Now take your hand off the cardboard. Record what happens.

Part C

1 Tie an inflated balloon to each end of a metric ruler. Tie a string to the middle of the ruler. Hold the string so that the ruler is suspended. Move the balloons in or out to balance the ruler.

2 Predict what will happen if one balloon is popped.

3 Using a straight pin, pop one balloon. *Safety Tip:* Be careful when using the straight pin.

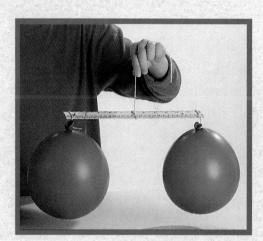

What Happened?

1. Compare your predictions with your observations in each part of the activity. How accurate were you?

2. Air pushes on things. It takes up space. Which two properties of air did you observe in Part A?

3. Which property of air did you observe in Part B?

4. Which properties of air caused the filled balloon to drop in Part C?

What Now?

1. Which property of air causes your ears to pop?

2. Which property of air helps you keep a bicycle tire inflated?

EXPLORE

The Properties of Air

Space

Were you surprised by any part of the Explore Activity? You know that air is matter. It has all the properties of matter. Did you believe that the air would keep water from flowing into the jar? Just like other matter, air took up the space in the jar and kept the water out.

Mass

Another property of matter is mass. Air also has mass. The inflated balloon in the Explore Activity was heavier than the empty, popped balloon. Which balloon had more matter? Which balloon had more mass?

CAREERS Blimp Pilot

If you have ever watched sports on TV, you've probably seen a view of the stadium from a blimp. **Blimps** are giant balloons that are filled with helium to make them lighter than air. To be a blimp pilot, you need a blimp license, and you should like to travel.

Blimp

Activity!

Massive Amounts of Air

To help you understand that air has mass, let's do the balloon part of the Explore Activity in a different way.

What You Need
balloon, balance, *Activity Log* page 4

Compare an empty balloon with one that is full of air. Do they have the same mass? First, use a balance to measure the mass of a balloon before it's inflated. Blow as much air into it as you can without breaking it. Use the balance to measure the mass of the balloon with the air inside. Subtract the mass of the empty balloon from the mass of the balloon with air. What is the mass of the air you breathed into the balloon?

Pressure

Like all matter, air has mass and takes up space. You can see how much space it takes up when you blow up a balloon. The difference in measurement between the empty balloon and the inflated balloon is the mass of the air. Now you will discover that air exerts pressure.

Minds On! Imagine you were at the bottom of a pile of feathers 10 meters (about 33 feet) deep. Would the feathers feel heavy to you? The pressure of the feathers would not push you down. Predict what you would feel if the feathers were piled up to 10 kilometers (about 6 miles). On the surface of Earth, you are at the bottom of a layer of air that is hundreds of kilometers deep. The weight of air pushing down on Earth's surface is **air pressure** (âr presh´ ər).

Activity!

Air Power

Did you know that you can lift heavy objects with air?

What You Need
plastic sandwich bag, plastic drinking straw, textbook, *Activity Log* page 5

Tape one end of the straw into the open end of the sandwich bag. Be sure the tape completely seals around the straw. You don't want any air passing in or out of the bag except through the straw. Set the bag under your textbook.

Blow into the straw with a steady, even breath. What do you notice about the book as you blow? Which of air's properties caused the change you saw? Record your observations or draw a picture of what you have just done in your *Activity Log.*

You saw how much power air has when it lifted your textbook. Rescue workers use air to lift a bus that has collided with a car.

If we measure air pressure at high altitudes, it is lower than at Earth's surface. Gravity holds most of Earth's air close to the surface. Gravity is less as you move farther from Earth's surface. If you go to higher altitudes, for example when you fly up in an airplane, there is less air above you so you feel less air pressure.

You have felt the change in air pressure if you have taken an elevator to the top of a tall building or flown in an airplane. Now that you know that air pressure is lower at high altitudes, can you explain why your ears pop on such rides?

The mercury barometer measures air pressure by using a hollow tube filled with mercury. Most weather stations and research laboratories use this barometer for accuracy.

The aneroid barometer also measures air pressure and is most often used in people's homes.

As the skydiver falls closer to Earth, the air pressure will increase.

The Atmosphere

Earth is surrounded by air just as your bed is covered by a blanket. This blanket of air is called the **atmosphere** (at´ məs fir´). Earth's atmosphere includes four layers. These layers have distinct characteristics.

The Northern Lights

In the high altitudes of the northern hemisphere, there is a natural light show that can be seen most easily at night. This display is called the **Northern Lights.** Sometimes the lights move or flicker far across the atmosphere for thousands of kilometers. The lights are usually blue-green, but sometimes they appear red or purple. There are similar lights in the high latitudes of the southern hemisphere called the Southern Lights.

The Northern and Southern Lights are the most visible evidence of the sun's effect on Earth's atmosphere.

Northern Lights

Ozone layer

weather balloon

cumulonimbus

Earth

weather satellite

The **exosphere** (ek´ sō sfîr´) is about 900 kilometers (about 560 miles) high. It is found at the edge of space.

These two sections of the atmosphere are often grouped together as the **thermosphere**.

meteors

The **ionosphere** (ī on´ ə sfîr´) is an upper layer of the atmosphere and is about 480 kilometers (about 298 miles) high. The air is very thin and there is very little gas in this layer.

The **mesosphere** (mez´ ə sfîr´) is the layer between 50 and 80 kilometers (about 50 miles) above the surface of Earth.

weather plane

The **stratosphere** (strat´ ə sfîr´) extends from the troposphere to about 50 kilometers (about 31 miles) above the surface of Earth. This is where transcontinental jet aircraft fly. It contains a region called the ozone layer, which absorbs ultraviolet rays from the sun.

cirrus

The layer closest to Earth is called the **troposphere** (trop´ ə sfîr´). This is the layer that contains the air and water that living things on Earth need to survive. The troposphere reaches to a height of about 13 kilometers (about 8 miles). The weather we experience in our everyday lives takes place in the troposphere.

Global Warming

Our atmosphere traps some of the solar energy that strikes Earth. We call this the **greenhouse effect**, and it helps keep Earth warm. One gas that helps trap this energy is carbon dioxide. If the amount of carbon dioxide increases, then we would expect the atmosphere to trap more heat. This would be an increase in the greenhouse effect, and it could cause Earth to get warmer. A worldwide increase in Earth's temperatures would be called **global warming**.

The glass or plastic of a greenhouse lets in sunlight. Some of the light is changed to energy that can't pass back through the glass, and this energy heats up the greenhouse.

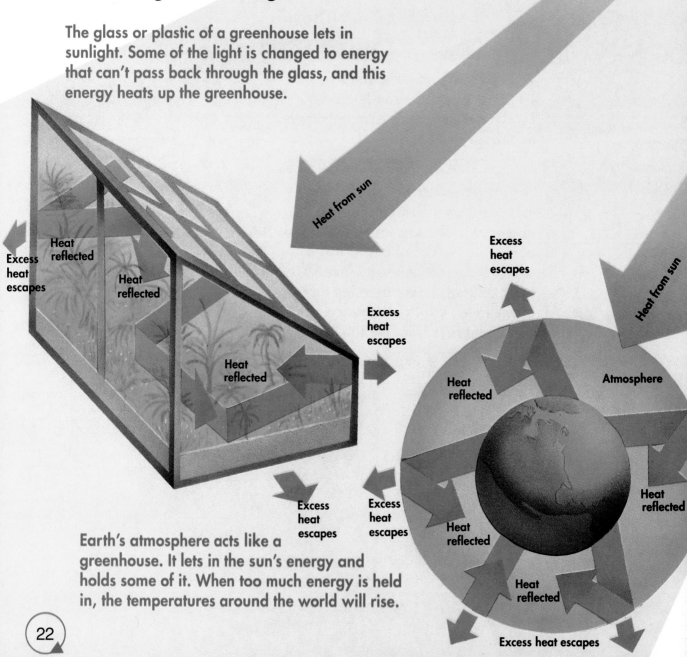

Heat from sun

Excess heat escapes

Heat reflected

Heat reflected

Heat reflected

Excess heat escapes

Excess heat escapes

Excess heat escapes

Excess heat escapes

Heat reflected

Heat from sun

Atmosphere

Heat reflected

Heat reflected

Heat reflected

Excess heat escapes

Earth's atmosphere acts like a greenhouse. It lets in the sun's energy and holds some of it. When too much energy is held in, the temperatures around the world will rise.

Minds On! What do you think would happen if Earth became warmer? Make a list of five good things and five problems that could happen as a result of global warming. ●

Much of the increase in carbon dioxide is caused by burning. People burn fuels in their automobiles, airplanes, and buses. Carbon dioxide also increases when there are fewer plants to take it out of the air. One method of clearing land for farming is to cut down all the trees and then burn the small plants that are left. In what two ways does this add carbon dioxide to the air?

Plant a tree to help absorb carbon dioxide. It will provide Earth with more oxygen.

Recycle aluminum cans, glass bottles, plastic products, and newspapers instead of throwing them away. It takes less energy to produce a new product from recycled materials.

Sum It Up

Excess heat escapes

Think of air as an invisible blanket that surrounds Earth. We call this the atmosphere. You can't see air, but you have proved that it is around you by investigating air's three properties. It has mass, it takes up space, and it exerts pressure. What else do you know about air? Just how important is it? Can you take air for granted?

Critical Thinking

1. Why is air pressure higher near Earth's surface than at altitudes farther away from Earth?
2. Why do your ears pop when you ride up or down in a fast elevator?
3. You have learned about three properties of air. Think of each property and give an example of each one that you use every day.

When you go to the grocery store, take a canvas or string bag with you.

Why Does the Wind Blow?

Have you felt the wind in your face or watched branches on a tree sway in the breeze? What causes the wind to blow? Why is the wind stronger on one day than it is on another?

About 500 years ago, seafarers were just beginning to understand how to find steady winds that always blew in the same direction. They gave names to these steady winds and marked them on charts, much as we mark highways on maps today.

In this lesson you'll learn what causes wind, how scientists measure wind speed and determine wind direction, and how people use wind for work and play. In the next activity, you'll build an instrument for measuring wind speed.

Minds On!

An international sign that warns residents who live near a coastal area that a hurricane is coming is two square red flags. The flags have black squares in the middle, and they fly one on top of the other. In the United States, these flags are flown from Coast Guard stations. Think of a flag that would warn people about dangerous wind conditions in your area. Where would you display this flag? Compare your idea with that of a classmate.

A ship sails on the Atlantic Ocean.

Activity!

Can You Measure Wind Speed?

Have you ever thought about how fast the wind blows on a very windy day? In the following activity, you will build an instrument that will measure the speed of the wind.

What You Need

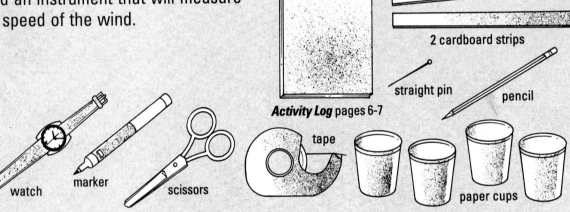

Activity Log pages 6-7

2 cardboard strips

straight pin

pencil

tape

paper cups

watch

marker

scissors

What To Do

1 Measure two lines 8 cm long on opposite sides of each cup. Cut carefully.

2 Mark one cup with a large black **X**.

Safety!

See the *Safety Tip* in step 5.

3 Make a plus sign with the strips of cardboard and tape them together.

4 Slide one of the cardboard strips' ends through the slits in each cup. All cups should face the same direction.

5 Push the straight pin through the center of the cardboard plus sign and into the eraser on the pencil. *Safety Tip:* Be careful when using the straight pin.

6 Draw a map of the schoolyard.

7 Holding on to the pencil securely, carry your device into the schoolyard. Observe what happens at four different locations. Choose locations near and away from buildings.

8 At each of the four locations that you have marked on your map, count the number of times the cup marked with the **X** spins past the holder's arm in 30 seconds. This number divided by 3 will give the approximate wind speed in kph. Write down the wind speed at each of the four locations on your map.

What Happened?

1. At which location did the wind blow the strongest?
2. At which location did the wind blow the least?

What Now?

1. Why do you think the wind speed was different in some of the locations where you tested your instrument?
2. List five activities or jobs that might be easier to do when the wind is blowing.

Which Way Does the Wind Blow?

In the Explore Activity, you made a weather instrument called an **anemometer** (an´ ə mom´ i tər). Your anemometer probably showed you that winds blew more briskly in certain locations. You might go to the same place tomorrow and find the wind blowing from another direction. Maybe the wind will not be as strong. Why does the wind have so little force one day and so much the next? To answer this question, you will need to learn more about temperature and air pressure. Differences in temperature and air pressure and the way they act together cause wind. **Wind** is the horizontal movement of air across Earth's surface.

Wind vanes point toward the direction from which the wind is blowing.

The water in the pool warms up more slowly than the land. It also cools more slowly. In the morning the water in the pool may be warmer than the concrete around the pool, because it has cooled more slowly during the night.

Activity!

Warming Up Fast or Slow

Try this activity to see if land really warms up more quickly than water.

What You Need

2 plastic boxes, water, sand, 16-oz. plastic jar, thermometer, *Activity Log* page 8

Place the two plastic boxes on the window sill where they will receive direct sunlight. Fill one box with a jar of sand and the other with a jar of water. Place a thermometer in each box every 10 minutes for a period of 30 minutes. Record the temperature in your ***Activity Log.*** In which material did the temperature rise faster? Now think about the air above the material. Predict which material would have warmer air above it. What does this activity show you about how the air above different surfaces on Earth is warmed?

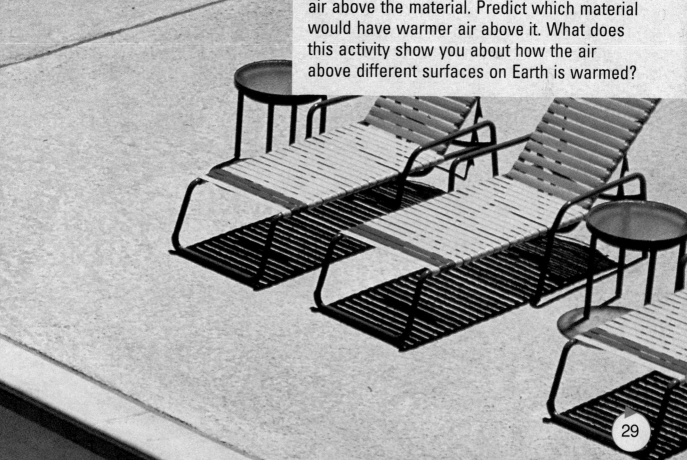

Why Breezes Blow

How do different temperatures in air cause wind? As air warms, its molecules move farther away from one another. If the molecules are farther apart, the air pressure is not as great. As air cools, the molecules move closer together. We say the air is **dense.** The more dense the air becomes, the more the pressure increases.

As the air gets warmer, it becomes less dense. It also has lower pressure than the air above the water.

The air above the shore also warms.

Winds form when the sun warms a surface, such as a shore near the ocean.

Winds begin to blow when cooler, more dense ocean air rushes in and pushes the warmer, less dense air up.

This cooler air is like the air let out of a balloon. It moves to an area of lower pressure. What do you think happens at night when the land becomes cooler than the water?

People have tried to control the wind for many reasons. Some people have used wind for transportation. Others use it to help make jobs easier. There are also some sports that use the wind.

Sailing for One

Focus on Technology

One wind sport that's become more popular in recent years is windsurfing. In addition to strong muscles and excellent swimming skills, you need an understanding of wind speed and direction to wind surf.

The person aboard grips a curved bar that moves the sail in any direction to take advantage of the wind.

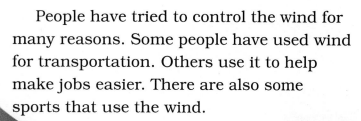

The sail is triangular and mounted on a mast that can tip and rotate. The sail uses the wind and helps steer the windsurfer.

A sailboard looks like a surfboard with a sail. One person rides it standing up.

Windmills in Holland were used to pump water from fields.

Focus on Technology

Wind Energy for the Future

As fuel supplies, such as coal, oil, and natural gas, become scarce and more expensive, people are again turning to an old source of energy. Wind machines are being used more and more.

Wind is a good source of energy for several reasons. First, energy from the wind is free, as long as you can catch it. Second, it is clean energy because it does not cause pollution. In areas where strong winds blow regularly, as in some valleys and deserts of California, the wind has become a reliable source of energy.

Sum It Up

From a soft, gentle breeze to a powerful hurricane, the wind is a part of everyday life. The wind can be a valuable resource when it is used to make jobs easier. Understanding how temperature and pressure work together to cause wind is important to understanding cycles in the atmosphere. In the next lesson, you'll discover how wind helps create weather patterns.

Critical Thinking

1. How does the sun affect the land and water to create wind?

2. Explain why winds near a large body of water blow toward the land during the daytime and toward the water at night.

3. Explain three ways wind could be used to do work.

Today's wind machines look like the windmills of old but are called wind turbines. Large blades collect the wind, and the turbine changes it into electricity.

Most of the wind energy collected is collected in California.

Windfarm, Altamont Pass, California, United States

How Does a Cloud Form?

Water is on Earth in lakes, rivers, oceans, and glaciers. After it rains we often see water in puddles. But a day or two after a rainstorm, the water in puddles has disappeared. Where does this water go?

Minds On! Think of three examples you have seen of disappearing water. Write these examples in your *Activity Log* on page 9. Explain what you think happened to the water.

Where Does the Water Go?

After it rains, water collects in streams that flow into rivers that in turn flow into the oceans. The oceans are very large, but why, after centuries of collecting water from rivers, don't they overflow?

Air contains oxygen, nitrogen, and small amounts of several other gases. One of those other gases is water vapor. Changing from a liquid to a gas is one of water's properties. In this lesson you'll learn how water travels from Earth up into the sky to become a cloud. You'll learn how clouds help us predict tomorrow's weather.

Grand Teton National Park
Wyoming, United States

Activity!

What Makes a Cloud?

A cloud may look fluffy and dry like cotton candy, but actually it is a million floating drops of water and, sometimes, ice crystals. How are clouds made?

What You Need

Activity Log pages 10-11

paper towel

water

ice

jar

What To Do

1 Wet the paper towel and wipe some water on the chalkboard. Watch the water, then record what happens to it in your *Activity Log.*

2 Half fill the jar with water. Look at the outside of the jar and then describe how it looks in your *Activity Log.*

3 Now add ice to fill the jar.

4 Continue to observe the jar. On the chart in your *Activity Log*, record changes that occur on the outside of the jar every 10 minutes for 30 minutes.

What Happened?

1. What did you see when you wiped the chalkboard with water?

2. What did you observe after you poured the water into the jar?

3. What about after you added the ice to the jar?

What Now?

1. Explain what happened to the water that was on the chalkboard.

2. Think back to the jar of ice and water—where did the water on the outside of the jar come from?

3. Some of the water on the outside of the jar was so heavy that it dripped down the jar. A ring or puddle formed around the jar on the table. Predict what would happen to the water in the puddle if you left it for two days. Record your prediction.

EXPLORE

The Water Cycle

In the Explore Activity, you saw water change from a liquid to a gas in the process called **evaporation** (i vap´ ə rā´ shən). The gas state of water is called water vapor. This is what happened when the water disappeared.

Adding ice to the water cooled the water and the jar. The water vapor near the jar cooled, also. It changed into water droplets. Changing from a gas to a liquid is called **condensation** (kon´ den sā´ shən). The droplets collected on the jar and clung to the sides. When the droplets became heavy and slid down the side of the jar, you saw another stage of the water cycle. **Precipitation** (pri sip´ i tā´ shən) happens when water falls from the sky in the form of rain, snow, hail, or sleet.

In Earth's water cycle, the sun is the energy source that causes evaporation.

Water condenses to form **clouds** of water droplets or ice particles suspended in the air.

The **water cycle** is the repeating cycle of evaporation, condensation, and precipitation that occurs on Earth.

The oceans do not overflow because water evaporates from them.

Rivers carry millions of liters of water into the oceans every day.

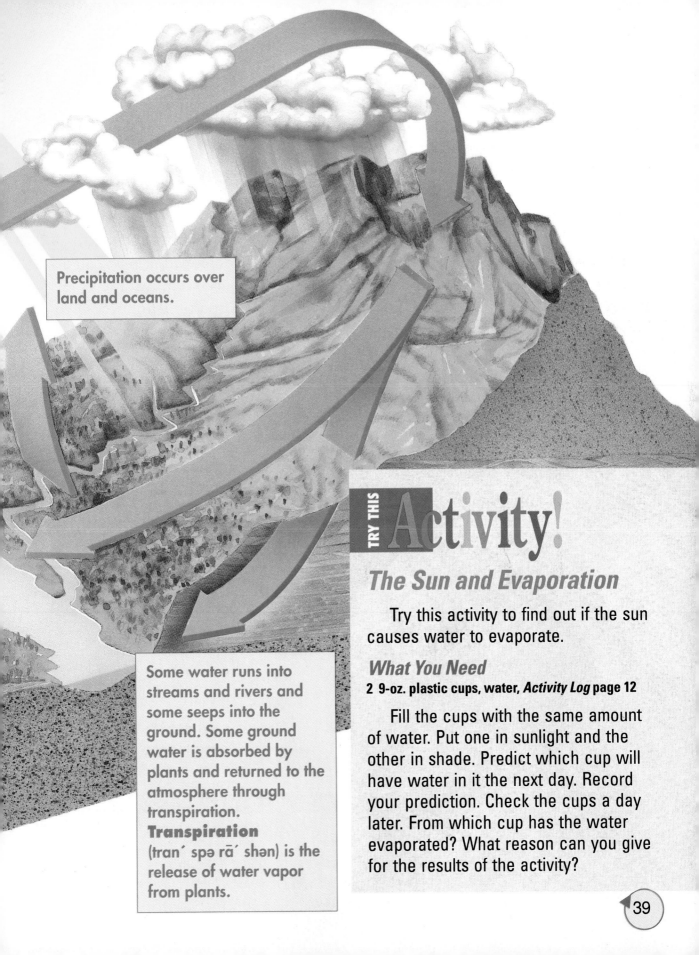

Precipitation occurs over land and oceans.

Some water runs into streams and rivers and some seeps into the ground. Some ground water is absorbed by plants and returned to the atmosphere through transpiration.

Transpiration (tran´ spə rā´ shən) is the release of water vapor from plants.

TRY THIS Activity!

The Sun and Evaporation

Try this activity to find out if the sun causes water to evaporate.

What You Need

2 9-oz. plastic cups, water, *Activity Log* page 12

Fill the cups with the same amount of water. Put one in sunlight and the other in shade. Predict which cup will have water in it the next day. Record your prediction. Check the cups a day later. From which cup has the water evaporated? What reason can you give for the results of the activity?

Minds On! You have been in a cloud-making chamber if you have ever taken a warm bath on a cold day. Once you've filled the tub with warm water, what do you see rising out of the water? What forms on the cold surfaces in the room, such as a mirror, a window, or tile walls? Describe the parts of the water cycle and where they are occurring in the bathroom. ●

The bathtub example shows us how water travels back to the air from the oceans. Ocean water is warmed by the sun until it evaporates and rises. High in the atmosphere, the air temperature is cooler, like the air temperature in your bathroom. Warm water vapor in the air condenses, or changes back into its liquid form, just as water vapor in the bathroom condensed on the mirror, window, or walls. The sun provides heat to cause evaporation. Where does the heat go?

The warm bath water evaporates and condenses to form water droplets because the air in the bathroom is cool and low in moisture.

Activity!

Cooling Off

In this activity you will discover where the heat goes.

What You Need

2 thermometers, wet paper towel, cardboard fan,
Activity Log **page 13**

Record the temperatures of the two thermometers in your *Activity Log.* Then, wrap the wet paper towel around the bulb of one thermometer. Leave the bulb of the other thermometer uncovered. Next, fan the bulbs of both thermometers with a cardboard fan for two minutes. Observe and record the temperatures of the thermometers. How did the temperatures change? Explain how a fan works to cool you on a hot summer day.

Health  Link

Nature's Air Conditioner

What happens when you run or play really hard? Do you sweat? Sweating helps cool you. Sweat evaporates from your skin and cools you just as the thermometer in the activity was cooled. When sweat evaporates, heat leaves your body and goes into the air.

Clouds

Have you ever been out and about on a foggy morning? Did it seem as if you had your head in the clouds? Actually you did, since fog is a cloud that has formed close to the ground. Fog is formed the same way as all other clouds are formed. When warm, moist air cools, the water vapor in the air condenses. When many millions of droplets form together, we see a cloud. In the case of fog, the warm, moist air cooled close to the ground instead of high in the atmosphere.

Cumulus (kū´ myə ləs) clouds are large, thick, and puffy. They often look white with gray centers. Cumulus clouds are usually flat on the bottom and pile up to look like a dome. These clouds often form on hot summer days and sometimes turn into thunderclouds or thunderheads. When this happens, rain or thunderstorms may occur.

Cirrus (sir´ əs) clouds are made of tiny ice crystals. They are thin and white with feathery edges. They are the highest clouds in the sky and are seen when the weather is cool and dry.

Stratus (stra´ təs) clouds form at low altitudes. They can hold a lot of moisture and spread across the sky in flat, gray layers.

Minds On! Have you ever watched the clouds float across the sky? Can you predict the weather from your observations? What type of cloud are you observing on a foggy morning? What weather will this type of cloud bring?●

TRY THIS

Activity!

Cloud Watching

Can you predict what tomorrow's weather will be by observing clouds?

What You Need
cotton balls, construction paper, glue, *Activity Log* page 14

From a window in your classroom, observe the clouds you can see. Use the cotton balls to make a model of the clouds you observe. Predict what you think tomorrow's weather will be based on the clouds you observe. Be sure to add these observations to your *Activity Log.* Check your prediction the next day.

Rain Shadow

Water is necessary for plants and animals to live and grow. Some areas of the world have lots of water. Other areas have little water because they get little rain. Some areas that are separated from an ocean by high mountains get little rainfall.

The air that moves over the mountain has little moisture left.

The water vapor in this air condenses and clouds form.

Rain or snow falls on the side of the mountain facing the ocean.

Moist air moving onto the land rises up the sides of the mountains. As it moves upward, it cools.

The land on the side of the mountain away from the ocean gets little rain. This area is called a **rain shadow,** a type of desert.

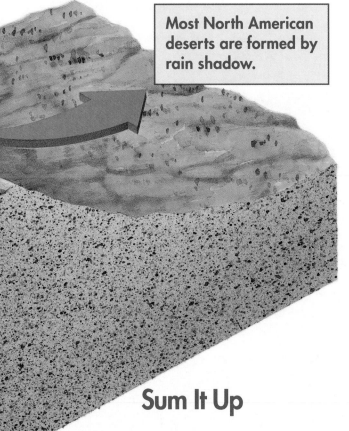

Most North American deserts are formed by rain shadow.

Making Deserts Green?

A **desert** is an area of land that receives less than 25 centimeters (about 10 inches) of rainfall per year. Very few plants grow in deserts because of the lack of water. In some places people have made desert areas green. They do this by bringing water to these areas. Watering this land by artificial methods is called **irrigation** (ir´ i gā´ shən). About 220 million **hectares** (about 550 million acres) of land are being irrigated around the world. In some countries more water is used for irrigation than for any other purpose.

Sum It Up

Understanding the water cycle will help you understand weather and how it changes. The water cycle is one of the cycles that are found in the different systems that form weather. For example, most storms are the result of the way that wind systems and water systems work together. Violent storms such as hurricanes bring both strong winds and heavy rains.

Critical Thinking

1. Why does fog often form early in the morning?

2. Why is your breath visible in cold weather?

3. On a hot day, someone sees you fanning yourself with a paper fan. This person says, "You're only making yourself hotter." How do you respond?

Why Does the Weather Change?

Whether the weather be fine
Or whether the weather be not
Whether the weather be cold
Or whether the weather be hot,
We'll weather the weather
Whatever the weather,
Whether we like it or not.

Changing weather in Loudoun County, Virginia, United States

Scientists who study the weather and prepare weather reports are called **meteorologists** (mē´ tē ə rol´ ə jists). One condition meteorologists use to help them forecast weather is air pressure. In the following activity, you will have a chance to make and use an instrument meteorologists use.

Activity!

Getting in Front of Weather Changes

In this activity you will make a weather instrument called a barometer and use it to observe changes in air pressure for four days. Using the barometer will help you predict the weather.

What You Need

Activity Log pages 15-16

safety goggles

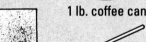
1 lb. coffee can

index card

rubber band   marker   balloon

tape

drinking straw

scissors

thermometer

What To Do

1 Cut the balloon just above the point where the neck ends. Stretch the balloon tightly over the open top of the can. Hold the balloon in place with a rubber band. *Safety Tip:* Wear safety goggles when using a rubber band.

2 Lay the drinking straw on the balloon so that about one-third of the straw sticks out beyond the edge of the can. Attach the straw to the balloon with a strip of transparent tape.

Safety!

See the *Safety Tip* in step 1.

3 Hold the index card lengthwise and write HIGHER at the top of the card and LOWER at the bottom of the card. Now fold the card lengthwise about 1 cm. Put a piece of masking tape on the fold and tape it just behind the part of the straw that is hanging over the edge of the can. At the end of the straw, mark the index card with a heavy black line and write DAY 1 next to the line.

4 Set up the thermometer near the barometer.

5 At the same time each day, mark the position of the straw on the card with a heavy black line and write DAY 2, DAY 3, DAY 4 so that you can see if the straw went up or down. Each day, record whether the pressure is rising or falling. Record the air temperature, sky color, clouds, and wind speed. Compare your observations with a newspaper or television weather report.

What Happened?

1. What happened to make your barometer record a high pressure on the card?

2. What type of weather did you see on days with high air pressure? What type of weather did you see on days with low air pressure?

3. Based on your observations in this activity, predict what weather conditions will be like on the fifth day.

What Now?

1. How accurate were your weather predictions?

2. What connection did you notice between air pressure and temperature?

3. What type of reading would you expect from your barometer if warm air were to move into your area?

EXPLORE

Air Masses and Fronts

Your barometer showed you changes in air pressure. When the air pressure fell, your barometer read lower. High air pressure made your barometer read higher.

Weather (weth´ ər) is the condition of the atmosphere at a particular time and place. When weather forecasters predict weather, they track the movement of air masses. An **air mass** is a large body of air with nearly the same temperature and moisture throughout. Air masses may form over either water or land. They take on the properties of the surfaces they form over.

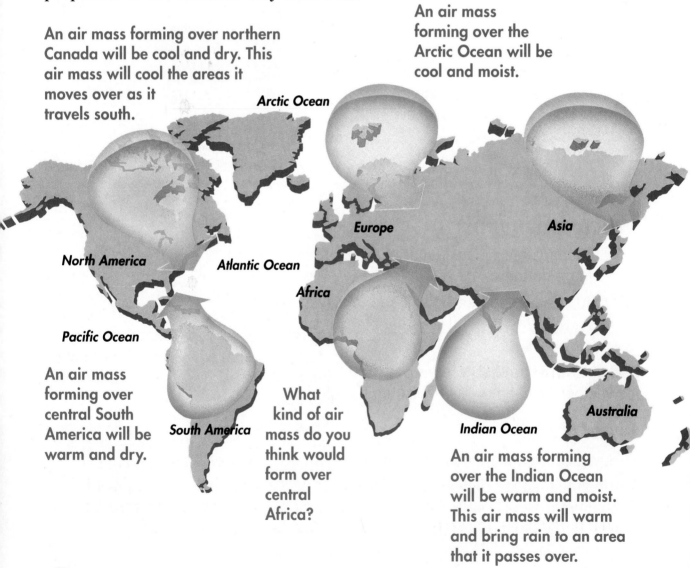

An air mass forming over northern Canada will be cool and dry. This air mass will cool the areas it moves over as it travels south.

An air mass forming over the Arctic Ocean will be cool and moist.

Arctic Ocean

Europe

Asia

North America

Atlantic Ocean

Africa

Pacific Ocean

An air mass forming over central South America will be warm and dry.

South America

What kind of air mass do you think would form over central Africa?

Indian Ocean

Australia

An air mass forming over the Indian Ocean will be warm and moist. This air mass will warm and bring rain to an area that it passes over.

Air masses move as the wind blows. When they move, they bump into or push against other air masses. Air masses usually do not mix because of differences in air pressure and temperature. The place where two different air masses meet is called a **front.** Most of our storms form along fronts.

A cold air mass moves through warm air.

A **cold front** often produces fast-rising air and strong winds. The dense cold mass slides under the less dense warm mass. This front may produce thunderstorms.

A warm air mass moves in an area of cool air.

Cirrus clouds may tell you a **warm front** is coming. In a warm front warm air rises up and over the denser cold air.

TRY THIS Activity!

Move Aside, Here I Come!

You are going to see how a front forms by using cold water and hot water.

What You Need
clear plastic shoe box, heavy piece of cardboard, red food coloring, blue food coloring, 16-oz. jar of very hot water, 16-oz. jar of very cold water, *Activity Log* page 17

Cut a heavy piece of cardboard so that it is exactly as wide as the shoe box. Place the cardboard across the middle of the shoe box vertically so that it divides the shoe box in half. It must fit very snugly. Ask your partner to hold the cardboard firmly in place. Put 5 drops of red food coloring in the jar of hot water that you have. Put 5 drops of blue food coloring in the jar of cold water. Swirl the jars to mix the food coloring with the water. *Safety Tip:* Pour the red water into one side of the box with care. Pour the blue water into the other side of the box. Have your partner quickly pull the cardboard straight up and out of the shoe box. What happened? Record your observations.

Thunderstorms

Minds On! Think about the last rainstorm in your area. Was the rain light and steady or heavy with strong winds, thunder, and lightning?

Rainstorms or snowstorms can happen when two air masses meet along a front. When the warm, humid air along a front is pushed up suddenly, a thunderstorm may develop.

As the warm air rises, it cools, and the water vapor condenses and forms a dark **thundercloud.** As more air is pushed up along the front, the cloud grows taller, forming a **thunderhead.**

Thunderheads can produce strong lightning, thunder, and heavy rains. Sometimes the water droplets fall to Earth as hail. Hail forms when water droplets in the thunderhead are moved quickly up and down through layers of cold air. The drops freeze into ice crystals and grow large enough to fall to the ground as lumps of ice.

Most thunderstorms in the United States occur from May through September. Thunderstorms can be very dangerous because the lightning that is produced from these storms can cause injury and sometimes death. Follow these safety tips if you know a thunderstorm is coming.

Weather   Literature Link

Read about severe weather storms in *Weather* by Howard E. Smith. As you read, make a list of the types of severe storms that occur in the world in your **Activity Log** on page 18. When you have finished reading, number the list of storms from most severe to least severe. Discuss the reasons for your choices with your classmates.

Never stand under a lone tree in an open field because lightning strikes the highest point around.

Don't stay outside during a storm. Go inside a large building or car to protect yourself from lightning.

Don't take a bath or shower. Stay away from water taps and sinks. Minerals in water conduct electricity from lightning, which could shock you.

Don't talk on the telephone unless it's an emergency. Telephone wires conduct electricity, and you could get a shock.

Tornadoes

The wind and lightning in thunderstorms can be very dangerous, but other storms can be even more violent. The **tornado** (tôr nā′ dō) is a rapidly circling column of air that moves in a narrow path over land. A tornado that is still in the air is called a funnel cloud.

A tornado can reach wind speeds of up to 418 kilometers (about 260 miles) per hour. It can pull up trees and tear apart buildings. Cars and trees have been lifted and carried through the air for hundreds of meters. Tornadoes kill many people because they appear so quickly and with less warning than other kinds of storms. A tornado is dangerous because it moves in an unpredictable path.

Tornadoes form in severe thunderstorms that contain rising warm air.

When the warm air rises in the back of the storm, it draws cool air from the bottom of the storm and forms funnel clouds.

Funnel clouds that touch the ground are called tornadoes.

More tornadoes occur in the United States than in any other country, especially in the area of the United States called Tornado Alley.

Tornadoes form when air masses of different temperatures collide. Most tornadoes occur from April through July. In the summer, in the states along Tornado Alley, hot land areas may warm up air masses throughout the day. In the late afternoon, as the temperature cools, cooler air masses may move in. Steep thunderheads will form along the cold front. Some thunderheads may extend upward to 1,825 meters (about 5,986 feet). In a thunderstorm system of this size, tornadoes may occur.

Hurricanes

If you live in a coastal area, you may have to prepare for hurricanes. A **hurricane** (hûr´ i kān´) is a violent storm that forms over a warm ocean. The official hurricane season in the United States is June 1 through November 30.

Winds swirl around the *eye*, or center, of the hurricane. The eye is actually a calm area with few clouds in which the sun may be shining. The eye measures about 32 kilometers (about 20 miles) in diameter.

Winds near the center of a hurricane range in speed from 119 to 322 kilometers (about 74 to 200 miles) per hour.

A hurricane usually measures from 322 to 805 kilometers (about 200 to 500 miles) in diameter.

Hurricanes form in areas of low pressure over warm water. Although they develop and pick up speed over water, hurricanes often move inland, away from the water.

When hurricanes move over coastal areas, the waves, tides, winds, and rain can cause enormous damage. The damage from a hurricane can extend over an area hundreds of kilometers from its center.

Wall clouds surround the eye of the hurricane. These clouds have the strongest winds and heaviest rain of the hurricane.

Hurricane!

Literature Link

Read Faith McNulty's book *Hurricane!* In your ***Activity Log*** on page 19, make a list of all the things John, his family, and the community do to prepare for the hurricane. Think about the kinds of buildings described in the book and what happens to them. What types of buildings can withstand hurricanes? What kinds of structures exist where you live? Add anything else you think you would need to do to prepare your home for a hurricane.

All in a Day's Work

Meteorologists around the world work together to share weather information gathered from satellites, weather balloons, radar, weather stations, aircraft, and computers.

Airline pilots radio air traffic control centers with the weather conditions of the air they are flying through.

Meteorologists use computers to gather weather data and make five-day forecasts.

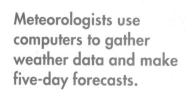

All around the world, gas-filled weather balloons are launched at midnight and midday to take measurements of air pressure, temperature, humidity, and wind speed at different levels of Earth's atmosphere.

Weather stations are used around the world to collect weather information every hour. Meteorologists use the data on wind speed and direction, air pressure, temperature, humidity, and precipitation to prepare forecasts.

There are two kinds of weather satellites that monitor cloud formations around the world. Meteorologists can predict what kind of weather is coming from the pictures sent back to Earth.

TRY THIS Activity! *Forecasting the Weather*

What You Need

4 days of newspaper weather maps, *Activity Log* page 20

A study of weather maps shows that weather fronts in the United States usually move from west to east. Use the newspaper weather maps to track an air mass in the United States for three days. In your *Activity Log,* record which states the air mass covered on each day. Write down if it is a warm or a cold air mass. Note any changes in size.

Predict where the air mass will move on the fourth day by drawing a map of the area it will cover. Prepare a weather forecast for that area. Compare your drawing with the newspaper map. How good was your weather forecasting?

Stormy Weather Worldwide

People around the world use many different words for the same weather conditions, especially for violent storms and winds.

Cyclone (sī´ klōn) comes from the Greek word *kykloein* (kü´ klō ān´), meaning "moving in a circle" or "whirling." In a cyclone, winds rotate around a moving center of low air pressure. Because of Earth's rotation, cyclones spin clockwise in the Southern Hemisphere and counterclockwise in the Northern Hemisphere. Hurricanes that form in the Indian Ocean are called cyclones.

Typhoon (tī fün´) takes us to the other side of the globe. It is from a Chinese word meaning "great wind." Hurricanes that form in the Pacific Ocean are called typhoons.

Monsoon (mon sün´) comes originally from an Arabic word meaning "season." Monsoons are the winds in the Indian Ocean that change direction with the season. They are very powerful, bring rain, and determine the time when the people can plant crops.

Santa Ana (san´ tə an´ ə) winds are named for the community of Santa Ana, California. They occur during the winter. They blow across the mountains from the deserts and plateaus of lower east California, carrying dust particles. They are hot and dry, and because they are so strong, they often make forest fires difficult to stop.

Sum It Up

The weather is always changing. Air masses and fronts move across Earth to cause all types of weather. The patterns of weather that forecasters track, plus weather instruments like barometers that forecasters use, work together to help people prepare for life-threatening storms as well as everyday weather.

Critical Thinking

1. What happens when two air masses meet?

2. How does a thunderhead develop?

3. How are tornadoes and hurricanes alike? How are they different?

Weather, Climate, and You

Do you have a different set of clothes for each season? Or can you wear the same type of clothing year-round? The weather and climate where you live affect what you do and what you wear all year long.

In some areas you can play on a beach in the winter.

Playing outdoors in the snow requires a hat, boots, mittens, and a heavy coat.

Meteorologists keep records of the weather in an area for about 30 years. They watch to see what kinds of weather occur over and over again. We call the pattern of weather in an area year after year the **climate** (klī´ mit). Climate affects your life in many ways. One of those ways is the clothing you wear. For example, if you live in Maine, you will need a heavy coat, mittens, boots, and a hat if you plan to play outdoors in the winter. If you live in Southern California, you might wear a light shirt and shorts in February!

You have been learning about weather conditions that happen day by day. Now you will study weather that happens over a longer period of time.

Activity!

Discovering Climate in North America

Many different climates exist in North America. You are going to investigate one area in North America and identify the type of climate in that area.

What You Need

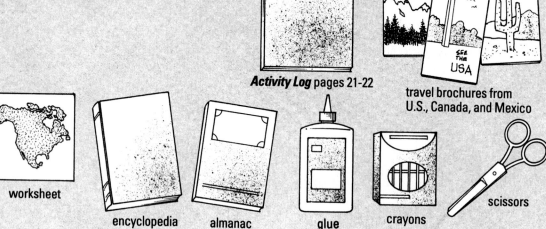

Activity Log pages 21-22

travel brochures from U.S., Canada, and Mexico

worksheet

encyclopedia

almanac

glue

crayons

scissors

What To Do

1 Look at the map of North America.

2 Color the zone marked *number 1,* blue. Color the zone marked *number 2,* green. Color the zone marked *number 3,* red.

3 Choose one of the areas that you just colored. Use the encyclopedia or travel brochures to find the average summer temperature and the average winter temperature in your zone of climate.

4 Use the encyclopedia or almanac to find the average yearly rainfall for your area.

5 Use the encyclopedia or travel brochures to find out what kinds of plants grow in your climate. Draw three kinds in your *Activity Log.*

6 Use the encyclopedia or travel brochures to find out what kinds of animals live in your climate zone. Draw one animal in your *Activity Log* or cut out a picture of one from a travel brochure.

What Happened?

1. What zone of climate would be the best for people who like winter sports?

2. Which zone of climate would be the best for farming?

3. How does the weather affect the way people live and work in the zone of climate you chose?

What Now?

1. What would happen to your area if the average yearly temperature increased?

2. What would happen to your area if the average yearly temperature decreased?

3. Does being close to or far away from the equator make a difference in the type of climate that an area has? Explain why you think so.

EXPLORE

World Climates

In the Explore Activity, you discovered that climate has an effect on plants, animals, and people. It makes a difference in the types of houses that people live in, the clothing they wear, the type of food they grow, and the jobs they do.

Laplanders live in a type of climate with long, bitterly cold winters and short, cool summers. Reindeer are raised for food and transportation.

Bedouins live in the deserts of the Middle East. They may live in tents and travel frequently to find water and grass for their camels, sheep, and goats.

People who live by the Mediterranean Sea usually have mild, rainy winters and hot summers. Anchovies, sardines, shrimp, and tuna are caught in the waters of the Mediterranean.

The Senegalese live on the tropical coast of Africa. The weather is usually warm and moist year-round.

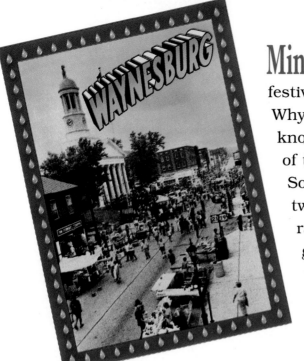

Minds On! Waynesburg, Pennsylvania, celebrates an interesting festival each July 29 called "Rain Day." Why is it always on July 29? No one knows why, but it has rained 95 out of the last 115 years on July 29. Sometimes it is just a sprinkle or two. Sometimes a downpour can rain the festival out! If you were going to celebrate a festival that was all about climate, what would it be? ●

Social Studies **62** Link

Let Us Plant Lettuce!

Have you ever helped someone plant seeds in a garden or a window box? What do you remember about the back of the seed package? Those multicolored maps are actually climate maps. The bands of color on the maps show the best time to plant the seeds in the packet for every area of the United States. The colors also show the last likely date for **frost** in an area. Farmers and gardeners need to know the frost date because frost will kill many vegetable and flower plants. What are the frost dates for your area? Can you grow vegetables year-round?

Seasons and Climates

You have learned that average temperature is related to geographic location. The way that Earth orbits around the sun should make this more clear for you.

Earth's axis is an imaginary line that runs through its center. The axis is always tilted in the same direction in space.

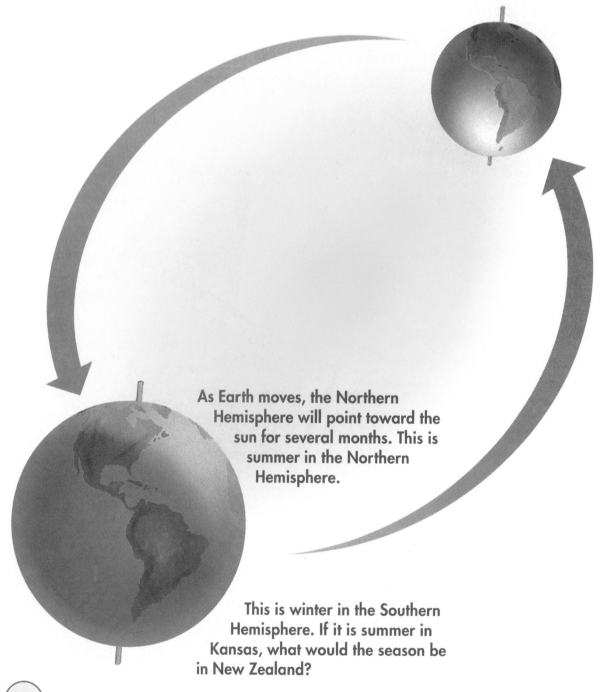

As Earth moves, the Northern Hemisphere will point toward the sun for several months. This is summer in the Northern Hemisphere.

This is winter in the Southern Hemisphere. If it is summer in Kansas, what would the season be in New Zealand?

Climate Zones

Earth has three basic climate zones—polar, tropical, and temperate. What climate zone do you live in?

Polar climates are cold and occur in regions that don't receive sunlight as directly as the tropical zone does.

Places closest to the equator have **tropical** climates. They are warm or hot year-round because they receive intense energy from the sun every day.

Places that are between the equator and the poles have **temperate** climates, which means that the weather is warmer than in the polar zone but cooler than in the tropical zone of climate.

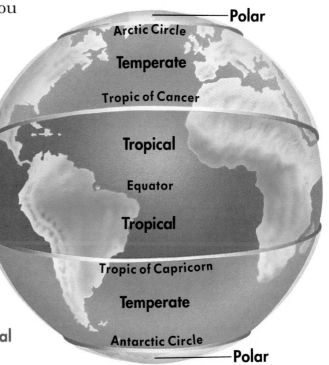

Polar

Arctic Circle

Temperate

Tropic of Cancer

Tropical

Equator

Tropical

Tropic of Capricorn

Temperate

Antarctic Circle

Polar

TRY THIS Activity! *Polar Zebra*

You have probably seen pictures of animals that live in a tropical climate. What would happen if a zebra or an elephant went to the North Pole to live?

What You Need
crayons, magazines or books with animal pictures, *Activity Log* page 23

Choose an animal that you know lives in a warm, tropical climate. Use the magazines or books to see where it lives. Think of three ways that the animal will have to adapt to a new, polar climate. Write the changes in your *Activity Log.* Draw a picture of the animal you have chosen in its new environment.

Repairing the Ozone

One place where scientists have carefully studied the atmosphere is over Antarctica. Some scientists are concerned about the holes that are growing in the ozone layer. **Ozone** (ō´ zōn) is a form of oxygen that can be found in the stratosphere. The ozone layer keeps out most of the sun's harmful **ultraviolet** (ul´ trə vī´ ə lit) rays, which can cause skin cancer. Scientists are also studying the effect of the holes on Earth's climate.

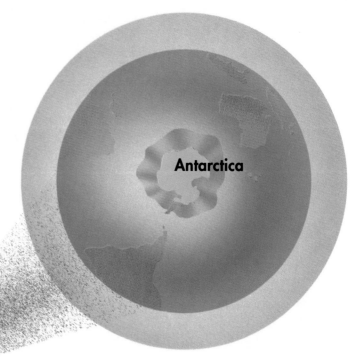

Antarctica

Scientists have found that the holes are caused by chemical compounds called **chlorofluorocarbons** (klôr´ ə flôr´ ə kär´ bənz) or CFCs. CFCs are used in refrigerators and in air conditioners for homes and cars. The United States and many other countries want CFCs to be eliminated in all products by the year 2000.

Aerosol cans, like the one shown here, contain CFCs, which harm the atmosphere. Most products now use air pump sprays.

Blocking Out the Sun

When you go outside to play on a sunny day, do you put sunblock on your face? Do you wear a hat? Do you rest in the shade or under an umbrella? When scientists became concerned about the amount of ultraviolet rays that were coming through the holes in the ozone layer, they advised people to use stronger protection for their skin. Have you seen sunscreen products that say SPF 15 or SPF 40 on the front? This means that the product you are using will give you 15 or 40 times more protection from the sun's ultraviolet rays than not using any protection at all. So be smart and protect your fragile skin when you play outdoors.

Always wear a sunscreen outdoors.

Sum It Up

Earth's climates are the result of many factors that work together. The climate where you live is a result of the weather that has happened for a long time, the distance you are from the equator, Earth's tilt, and whether you live near a large body of water or near mountains or hills. Where you live affects the way you live. How does climate affect your life?

Critical Thinking

1. Geographical location is important to the climate of an area. Think of some landforms that influence your climate.

2. How do air temperature and ground surface work together to cause climate?

3. Draw three ways that people can affect the climate around them. Make your drawings colorful and eye-catching.

Understanding Air, Weather, and Climate

You know that weather and climate are both caused by the interaction between the sun and Earth. The daily changes that take place in the troposphere are called weather. Climate is the average weather of an area measured over a longer period of time. What do weather and climate have in common? Wind, temperature, and water are three important conditions for weather and climate.

Worldwide Weather Disasters

Social Studies Link

You have seen that weather can be unpredictable even though meteorologists have the most modern scientific equipment to track storms around the world. Here are some weather disasters that happened from 1737 to the present day. After you have read the time line, decide if you think any of these events could have been prevented. Choose one of the events on the time line and find out more about the disaster. What makes one disaster worse than another?

1737 India

A giant storm surge caused by a tropical cyclone swept away everything in its path on the Hooghly (hü´ lē) River.

1876–1879 China

Crop failure caused by lack of rain resulted in the Great Famine.

1899 United States

A dam at the head of the South Fork Reservoir, in a valley of the Allegheny Mountains, burst after a long period of rain and flooded Johnstown, Pennsylvania.

1954 Austria

An avalanche traveling at a speed of more than 320 kilometers (about 200 miles) per hour roared down Mt. Montcalv (män käl´) and buried the town of Blons (blônz).

1954 Haiti

Hurricane Hazel blew winds of over 192 kilometers (about 119 miles) per hour over Haiti's southern coast.

1962 Peru

Unusually warm temperatures melted a glacier on top of Nevado Huascaran (nä vä´ do hwa skä rän´). A wall of ice and snow crashed down on the town of Ranrahirca (rän rä´ hîr kä) at more than 161 kilometers (about 100 miles) per hour.

1991 Bangladesh (bang glə desh´)

Islands were covered by a 6-meter (about 20 feet) tidal wave.

Activity!

As the World Turns

Climate is different all around the world. What makes it that way? Read these interesting facts about climate. Write your answers to the following questions in your *Activity Log.*

What You Need
meter tape, atlas, globe, *Activity Log* page 24

Greatest number of thunderstorm days: Kampala, Uganda 242 thunderstorm days per year

What do you think the climate is like in Kampala?

Greatest rainfall in one year: 2,602 centimeters Assam, India August 1860 to August 1861

With the meter tape, measure out 2,602 centimeters. Where do you think all the water would go?

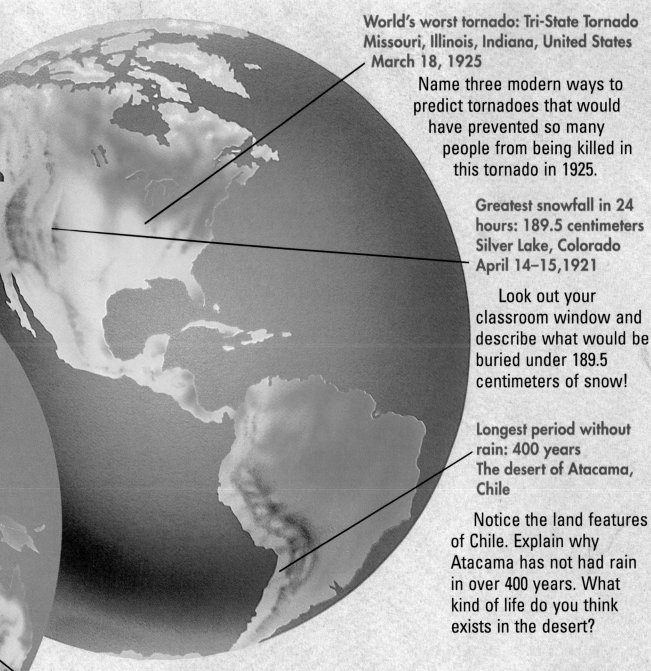

World's worst tornado: Tri-State Tornado
Missouri, Illinois, Indiana, United States
March 18, 1925

Name three modern ways to predict tornadoes that would have prevented so many people from being killed in this tornado in 1925.

Greatest snowfall in 24 hours: 189.5 centimeters
Silver Lake, Colorado
April 14–15, 1921

Look out your classroom window and describe what would be buried under 189.5 centimeters of snow!

Longest period without rain: 400 years
The desert of Atacama, Chile

Notice the land features of Chile. Explain why Atacama has not had rain in over 400 years. What kind of life do you think exists in the desert?

Longest hot spell: 38°C for 162 consecutive days
Marble Bar, Western Australia
October 31, 1923, to April 7, 1924

What kinds of activities could you do if there were no air conditioning or public pools to keep you cool during a heat wave?

Minds On! Imagine you could choose to live in any area on Earth. Where do you think is the perfect place? List three reasons for choosing this area. Describe the climate of your new home in a picture.●

GLOSSARY

Use the pronunciation key below to help you decode, or read, the pronunciations.

Pronunciation Key

a	at, bad	d	dear, soda, bad
ā	ape, pain, day, break	f	five, defend, leaf, off, cough, elephant
ä	father, car, heart	g	game, ago, fog, egg
âr	care, pair, bear, their, where	h	hat, ahead
e	end, pet, said, heaven, friend	hw	white, whether, which
ē	equal, me, feet, team, piece, key	j	joke, enjoy, gem, page, edge
i	it, big, English, hymn	k	kite, bakery, seek, tack, cat
ī	ice, fine, lie, my	l	lid, sailor, feel, ball, allow
îr	ear, deer, here, pierce	m	man, family, dream
o	odd, hot, watch	n	not, final, pan, knife
ō	old, oat, toe, low	ng	long, singer, pink
ô	coffee, all, taught, law, fought	p	pail, repair, soap, happy
ôr	order, fork, horse, story, pour	r	ride, parent, wear, more, marry
oi	oil, toy	s	sit, aside, pets, cent, pass
ou	out, now	sh	shoe, washer, fish mission, nation
u	up, mud, love, double	t	tag, pretend, fat, button, dressed
ū	use, mule, cue, feud, few	th	thin, panther, both
ü	rule, true, food	th	this, mother, smooth
ú	put, wood, should	v	very, favor, wave
ûr	burn, hurry, term, bird, word, courage	w	wet, weather, reward
ə	about, taken, pencil, lemon, circus	y	yes, onion
b	bat, above, job	z	zoo, lazy, jazz, rose, dogs, houses
ch	chin, such, match	zh	vision, treasure, seizure

air mass (âr mas) a body of air with about the same temperature, humidity, and pressure

air pressure (âr presh´ər) the pressure exerted in all directions by air pressing on an object

anemometer (an´ə mom´i tər) weather instrument that measures wind speed

atmosphere (at´məs fîr´) gases surrounding Earth

barometer (bə rom´i tər) instrument for measuring air pressure

blimp (blimp) airship with no rigid framework

chlorofluorocarbon (klôr´ə flür ə kär´bən) any of various compounds made of carbon, chlorine, fluorine, and sometimes hydrogen

cirrus (sir´əs) white, wispy, high-level cloud made up of ice crystals

climate (klī´mit) the typical weather conditions of a particular place over a long period of time

cloud (kloud) a mass of water droplets and/or ice particles floating in the air

cold front (kōld frunt) the forward edge of a mass of cold air moving into an area of warmer air

condensation (kon´den sā´shən) the change of a gas into a liquid or solid

cumulus (kū´myə ləs) a dense cloud made up of billowing mounds

cyclone (sī´klōn) a disturbance in the atmosphere in which winds rotate around a low air pressure center

dense (dens) having parts closely packed together

desert (dez´ərt) region with less than 25 centimeters (about 10 inches) of rainfall annually

evaporation (i vap´ə rā´shən) the change of a liquid into a gas

front (frunt) the boundary between two air masses of different temperature

frost (frôst) tiny ice crystals that form when water vapor changes directly to ice on the surface of exposed objects

global warming (glō´bəl wôrm´ing) a rise in Earth's average temperatures

greenhouse effect (grēn´hous´ i fekt´) a warming process in which the sun's heat is temporarily trapped in the atmosphere by certain atmospheric gases such as water vapor, carbon dioxide, and methane

hectare (hek´târ) a unit of area in the metric system, equal to 10,000 square meters or about 2½ acres

hurricane (hûr´i kān´) a storm of tropical origin with winds of about 121 kilometers (about 75 miles) per hour or more in the Atlantic and Caribbean regions

ionosphere (ī on´ə sfîr´) an area of ionized gases high in Earth's atmosphere

irrigation (ir´i gā´shən) bringing water to crops by artificial means

mass (mas) the amount of matter in an object

mesosphere (mez´ə sfîr´) the layer of Earth's atmosphere above the stratosphere

meteorologist (mē´tē ə rol´ə jist) a scientist who studies the weather

monsoon (mon sün) a seasonally varying wind of the Indian Ocean and southern Asia.

ozone (ō´zōn) a form of oxygen that is a pale blue gas with a distinctive odor

ozone layer (ō´zōn lā´ər) a layer of ozone in the stratosphere which absorbs ultraviolet rays, preventing them from reaching Earth

precipitation (pri sip´i tā´shən) any form of water that falls to Earth

rain shadow (rān shad´ō) a dry area on the downward side of a mountain

Santa Ana (San´tə an´ə) seasonal winds that blow in California

stratosphere (strat´ə sfîr´) the layer of the atmosphere above the troposphere, where a major ozone layer occurs

stratus (strā´təs) a low-level gray cloud that has a flat, layered form

thundercloud (thun´dər kloud) a large, dark cloud charged with electricity and producing thunder and lightning

thunderhead (thun´dər hed) upper portion of a thundercloud

tornado (tôr nā´dō) severe funnel shaped storm in which winds blow very rapidly around an area of very low pressure

transpiration (tran´spə rā´shən) the process by which plants transfer water vapor to the atmosphere

troposphere (trop´ə sfîr´) the layer of the atmosphere closest to Earth

warm front (wôrm frunt) the forward edge of a mass of warm air that is rising over a mass of cold air

water cycle (wô´tər sī´kəl) the continuous movement of water in the environment through evaporation, condensation, and precipitation

weather (weth´ər) the day to day conditions in the atmosphere, such as temperature, wind speed and direction, air pressure, humidity, and precipitation

wind (wind) air moving through the atmosphere

INDEX

Air, 12-23, 35; *act.,* 14-15, 17, 20; atmosphere, 20-23, 72; *illus.,* 21; carbon dioxide, 12, 22-23; dense, 30; helium, 16; nitrogen, 12, 35; oxygen, 12, 23, 35, 70; properties of, 16-19; water vapor, 35, 38, 40, 42, 44, 52

Air masses, 50-52, 55, 59; *illus.,* 50

Air pressure, 17-19, 28, 30, 33, 46-51, 56, 58-59; *act.,* 18, 48-49; *illus.,* 18-19

Altitude, 19

Anemometers, 28, *act.,* 26-27

Ardley, Neil, 11

Atmosphere, 20-23; *illus.,* 20-21; exosphere, 21; ionosphere, 21; mesosphere, 21; troposphere, 21, 72; stratosphere, 21, 70

Avalanches, 73

Axis of Earth, 68; *illus.,* 68

Barometers, 8, 19; *act.,* 48-49; *illus.,* 8, 19

Blimps, 16; *illus.,* 16-17

Book reviews, 10-11

Branley, Franklin M., 11

Carbon dioxide, 12, 22-23

Chlorofluorocarbons, 70; *illus.,* 70

Christian, Mary Blont, 11

Cirrus clouds, 42, 51; *illus.,* 42-43, 51

Climate, 62-69, 72-75; *act.,* 64-65, 74-75; *illus.,* 66-69; zones, 69; *act.,* 69; *illus.,* 69

Clouds, 21, 34-35, 42-43, 59; *act.,* 36-37, 40, 43; cirrus, 42, 51; *illus.,* 42-43, 51; cumulus, 42; *illus.,* 42; fog, 42-43; funnel, 54-55; *illus.,* 54-55; stratus, 43; *illus.,* 42-43; thunderclouds, 52; wall, 57; *illus.,* 57

Cold front, 51

Computers, 58

Condensation, 38, 40, 42, 44, 52

Cumulus clouds, 42; *illus.,* 42

Cyclones, 60, 72; *illus.,* 60, 72

Deserts, 45

Evaporation, 38-41; *act.,* 39, 41

Exosphere, 21; *illus.,* 21

Fog, 42-43

Fronts, 51, 59; *act.,* 51; *illus.,* 51

Frost, 67

Funnel clouds, 54-55; *illus.,* 54-55

Glaciers, 73; *illus.,* 73

Global warming, 22-23; *act.,* 23; *illus.,* 22

Gravity, 19

Greenhouse effect, 22; *illus.,* 22

Hail, 52

Hectare, 45

Helium, 16

Hemispheres, 68; *illus.,* 68

Humidity, 58-59

***Hurricane!* (McNulty),** 10, 57

Hurricanes, 10-11, 24, 56-57, 73; *illus.,* 56-57, 73; eyes of, 56; *illus.,* 56

Ionosphere, 21; *illus.,* 21

Irrigation, 45

Lightning, 52-54

Mass, 16-17; *act.,* 17

Matter, 16-17

McNulty, Faith, 10, 57

Mesosphere, 21; *illus.,* 21

Meteorologists, 47, 58-59; *illus.,* 46-47, 58-59

Monsoons, 61; *illus.,* 61

Mountains, 44-45; *illus.,* 44-45

Mystery of the Double Double Cross, The **(Christian),** 11

Nitrogen, 12, 35

Northern Lights, 20-21; *illus.,* 20-21

Orbit of Earth, 68; *illus.,* 68

Oxygen, 12, 23, 35, 70

Ozone layer, 21, 70-71; *illus.,* 70

Polar zones, 69; *act.,* 69; *illus.,* 69

Precipitation, 38-39; hail, 52; rain, 8, 34, 42-45, 52, 57, 61, 72-73; *illus.,* 44-45, 61, 72-73; snow, 6, 44, 52, 75

Pressure, 17-19, 28, 30, 33, 46-51, 56, 58-59; *act.,* 48-49

Radar, 58

Rain, 8, 34, 42-45, 52, 57, 72-73; *illus.,* 44-45, 72-73; monsoons, 61; *illus.,* 61; shadow, 44-45; *illus.,* 44-45

Santa Ana winds, 61; *illus.,* 61

Satellites, 58-59; *illus.,* 59

Science Book of Air, The **(Ardley),** 11

Simon, Seymour, 11

Smith, Howard E., 53

Snow, 6, 44, 52, 75

Solar Energy, 22

Storms **(Simon),** 11

Storms, 6-18, 51-57; cyclones, 60, 72; *illus.,* 60, 72; hurricanes, 10-11, 56-57, 73; *illus.,* 56-57, 73; monsoons, 61; *illus.,* 61; Santa Ana winds, 61; *illus.,* 61; thunderstorms, 6, 11, 42, 51-55; *illus.,* 51-53; tornadoes, 11, 54-55, 75; *illus.,* 54-55; typhoons, 60; *illus.,* 60

Stratosphere, 21, 70; *illus.,* 21

Stratus clouds, 42-43; *illus.,* 42-43

Temperate zones, 69; *illus.,* 69

Temperature, 9, 19-20, 28-30, 33, 50-51, 58-59, 68; *act.,* 29

Thermometers, 9, 41, *illus.,* 9

Thunderclouds, 52

Thunderheads, 52, 55

Thunderstorms, 6, 11, 42, 51-55; *illus.,* 51-53

Tidal waves, 73; *illus.,* 73

Tides, 57

Tornado Alert **(Branley),** 11

Tornado Alley, 55; *illus.,* 55

Tornadoes, 11, 54-55, 75; *illus.,* 54-55

Transpiration, 39

Tropical zone, 69; *act.,* 69; *illus.,* 69

Troposphere, 21, 72; *illus.,* 21

Typhoons, 60; *illus.,* 60

Ultraviolet rays, 21, 70-71

Wall clouds, 57; *illus.,* 57

Warm front, 51

Water, 29-30, 34-40; cycle, 38-40, 45; *act.,* 36-37, 39; *illus.,* 38-39; vapor, 35, 38, 40, 42, 44, 52

Weather **(Smith),** 11, 53

Weather, 46-69, 72-75; *illus.,* 74-75; air masses, 50; *illus.,* 50; air pressure, 17-19, 28, 30, 33, 46-51, 56, 58-59; *act.,* 48-49; climate, 63-69, 72-75; *act.,* 64-65, 74-75; *illus.,* 66-69; disasters, 72-73; *illus.,* 72-73; fog, 42-43; fronts, 51; frosts, 67; humidity, 58-59; precipitation, 6, 8, 34, 38-39, 42-45, 52, 57, 61, 72-73; *act.,* 6; *illus.,* 44-45, 61, 72-73; predicting, 35, 43, 59; *act.,* 43, 48-49, 59; storms, 6-8, 42, 51-57, 60-61, 72-73, 75; *illus.,* 51-57, 60-61, 72-73; temperature, 9, 19-20, 28-30, 33, 50-51, 58-59, 68-69, 75; *act.,* 29; winds, 24-33, 54, 57-59, 60-61, 72; *act.,* 26-27; *illus.,* 8, 30-33, 60-61, 72

Weather balloons, 58; *illus.,* 58

Windmills, 33; *illus.,* 33

Winds, 24-33, 54, 57-59; *act.,* 26-27, 29; *illus.,* 8, 30-33; cyclones, 60, 72; *illus.,* 60, 72; energy, 32-33; Santa Ana, 61; *illus.,* 61; typhoons, 60; *illus.,* 60

Windsurfing, 31; *illus.,* 31

Wind turbines, 32-33; *illus.,* 32-33

CREDITS

Contents

What Are Mountains? 4

Why Are Mountains Important? 7

What's Green and Growing in the Mountains? 10

What Animals Live in the Mountains? 14

How Do Animals Live in Mountains? 17

What's for Dinner in the Mountains? 19

How Do Mountain Animals Get Food? 21

How Do Mountains Affect People? 24

How Do People Affect Mountains? 26

Fact File 28

Glossary 30

More Books to Read 31

Index 32

What Are Mountains?

Bear Mountain in New York is 1,200 feet (366 meters) tall. Mount Everest in Nepal is 29,108 feet (8,872 meters) tall. Both of these are mountains. A mountain is a landform that rises at least 1,000 feet (300 meters) above the surrounding land. Every continent on Earth has mountains.

Mountains form in different ways

Strong movements of the earth under the ground form mountains. The force of these movements pushes rock layers upward. Volcanic mountains form when molten rock forces its way to Earth's surface.

A group of mountains is called a **range.** The Rocky Mountains in North America and the Andes in South America are mountain ranges. So are the Alps in Europe and the Himalayas in Asia.

> Africa's tallest mountain is Mount Kilimanjaro in Tanzania. It is not part of a mountain range. It is a single volcanic mountain.

❓ Did you know?

A mountain is measured by its **altitude.** This is how high it is above the ocean or sea level.

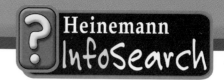

Living on a

Mountain

Heinemann Library
Chicago, Illinois

Carol Baldwin

Customer Service 888-454-2279

Visit our website at www.heinemannlibrary.com

Designed by Kimberly Saar, Heinemann Library
Illustrations and maps by John Fleck
Photo research by Alan Gottlieb
Printed and bound in the United States by Lake Book Manufacturing, Inc.

08 07 06 05 04
10 9 8 7 6 5 4 3 2 1

Library of Congress Cataloging-in-Publication Data
Baldwin, Carol.
  Living on a mountain / Carol Baldwin.
    v. cm. -- (Living habitats
Includes bibliographical references and index.
Contents: What are mountains? -- Why are mountains important? -- What's green and growing in the mountains? -- What animals live in the mountains? -- How do animals live in the mountains? -- What's for dinner in the mountains? -- How do mountain animals get food? -- How do mountains affect people? -- How do people affect mountains?
  ISBN 1-4034-2993-6 (Library Binding-hardcover) -- ISBN 1-4034-3233-3 (Paperback)
  1. Mountain ecology--Juvenile literature. [1. Mountains. 2. Mountain ecology. 3. Ecology.] I. Title.
  QH541.5.M65B35 2003
                    577.5'3--dc21

Acknowledgments
The author and publishers are grateful to the following for permission to reproduce copyright material:
p. 4 Sharna Balfour/Gallo Images/Corbis; p. 5 James L. Amos/Corbis; p. 7 Kevin and Betty Collins/Visuals Unlimited; p. 8 Randall J. Hodaes/Bruce Coleman Inc.; p. 9 George Gerster/NMR; p. 10 Hubertus Kanus/Photo Researchers, Inc.; p. 11 Tom Kloster; p. 12 Joy Spurr/Bruce Coleman Inc.; p. 13 Wolfgang Kaehler/Corbis; p. 14 Tom McHugh/Photo Researchers, Inc.; p. 15 Anthony Mercieca Photo/Photo Researchers, Inc.; p. 16 Tom and Pat Leeson/Photo Researchers, Inc.; p. 17 Galen Rowell/Corbis; p. 18 Mark Boulton/Photo Researchers, Inc.; p. 19 Walt Anderson/Visuals Unlimited; p. 20 Craig K. Lorenz/Photo Researchers, Inc.; p. 21 Jeff Lepore/Photo Researchers, Inc.; p. 22 Photo Researchers, Inc.; p. 24 Bruce Coleman Inc.; p. 25 AP/Wide World Photos; p. 26 M.F. Soper/Bruce Coleman Inc.; p. 27 Phil Schermeister/Corbis.

Cover photograph by Tui De Roy/Roving Tortoise Photography

About the cover: The Andean condor is native to South America. It is the largest bird of prey in the world. It has a wingspan of ten feet, stands four feet (1.2 meters) tall, and can weigh 30 pounds (13.6 kilograms).

Some words are shown in bold, **like this**. You can find out what they mean by looking in the glossary.

The Appalachians were once more than 13,000 feet (3,960 meters) high. But more than 250 million years of **erosion** have worn them down. Now the tallest peak is only 6,684 feet (2,037 meters) high.

Mountains change over time

Most mountains formed millions of years ago. Over time, some mountains get shorter. Ice, wind, and rain wear them down. North America's Appalachians and the Urals in Russia are lower now than they used to be. Volcanic mountains sometimes explode. Mount St. Helens in Washington lost its top and one side this way. Other mountains grow because of movements in Earth's crust. The Himalayas are growing about 3.3 feet (1 meter) every thousand years.

Paricutin

In 1943, a Mexican farmer saw the ground in his cornfield crack open. Smoke and ash started coming from the crack. The ground started to rise. Paricutin volcano was forming. The volcano continued to grow for eight years. It formed a mountain 1,100 feet (336 meters) high the first year. In the next seven years, it grew another 290 feet (88 meters).

Mountains have different life zones

As you travel up a mountain, it gets colder. The temperature drops about 3 °F (1.7 °C) for every 1,000 feet (348 meters) you go up. The air becomes thinner and there is not as much oxygen in it. The wind also blows harder. These changes affect the kinds life found in different areas, or zones, on the same mountain. Most mountains have several **life zones.** Each zone contains different kinds of plants and animals. Only plants and animals **adapted** to the **habitat** can live in each zone. For example, in the Alps of Europe, forests of **broad-leaved** trees grow at the base of mountains. Forests of pines and other **evergreens** grow higher on the mountain where it is colder. Only plants adapted to the cold can grow still higher on the mountain. On the mountain top, there is only snow and bare rock.

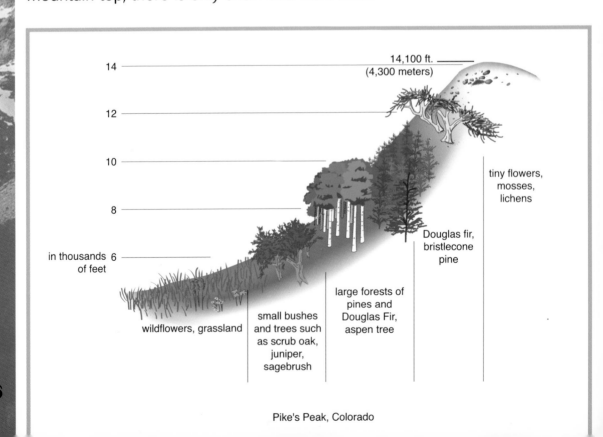

14,100 ft.
(4,300 meters)

14

12

10

8

in thousands 6
of feet

tiny flowers,
mosses,
lichens

Douglas fir,
bristlecone
pine

large forests of
pines and
Douglas Fir,
aspen tree

wildflowers, grassland

small bushes
and trees such
as scrub oak,
juniper,
sagebrush

Pike's Peak, Colorado

Why Are Mountains Important?

These fields in Peru's Andes Mountains, which were cut like steps, have been farmed for at least a thousand years.

Mountains have many different habitats. This allows many different plants and animals to live on mountains. People live in mountain **ranges** and use the mountains' **resources.**

People live on mountains

Mountains are home to many people. Incas and other Indian cultures have lived in the Andes for thousands of years. Large cities are also found in mountains. Quito, Ecuador, is in the Andes. Bern, Switzerland, is in the Alps. And Denver, Colorado, is in the Rocky Mountains. Because the Himalayas are so high, most people live in valleys between mountain peaks.

Mountains form natural borders

Some mountains separate countries. The Pyrenees separate France and Spain. The Andes separate Chile and Argentina. Others divide continents. The Urals divide Europe from Asia.

? Did you know?

La Paz, Bolivia, is the world's highest capital city. It is located nearly 12,000 feet (3,660 meters) high in the Andes Mountains.

Mountains affect climate

Mountains can affect the **climates** of lowlands around them. One example is what happens along the west coasts of North and South America. In both places, damp air blows from the Pacific Ocean onto the land. In the northwestern United States, the air runs into the Cascade Mountain **range.** In South America, it runs into the Andes. When the damp air reaches the mountains, it rises and cools. Clouds form and heavy rains fall on the western slopes. Forests can grow here. When the air reaches the mountains' eastern sides, it is dry. Very little rain falls here. This is called the rain shadow effect. Some of Earth's driest deserts are separated from wet forests by only a few hundred miles.

Land to the east of the Cascade Mountains in Washington does not get much rain. So only plants like sagebrush are able to grow there.

Mountains have mineral resources

Mountains have been the source of **minerals** for centuries. Indians of South America mined gold in the Andes for hundreds of years. But now mostly copper and tin are mined in the Andes. Russians mine iron, copper, and zinc in the Ural Mountains. Austrians mine salt in the Alps. Copper, gold, and silver are mined in the Rocky Mountains of North America.

Mountains are home to living things

Because mountains have different **life zones**, they have great **biodiversity.** That means they are home to many different **species** of life. Some of these living things are found nowhere else on Earth.

This salt mine is located in mountains near Nordrhein Westphalia in Germany. It is the largest salt mine in the world.

? Did you know?

Salzburg means "salt city." Salzburg, Austria, got its name from the nearby salt mines. Money from the sale of salt let the city build grand churches and palaces.

9

3 What's Green and Growing in the Mountains

Different plants grow at different levels of a mountain. The plants are **adapted** to the temperatures and rainfall at each level.

Plants at low altitudes

Forests of **broad-leaved** trees, such as oaks and maples, grow at the bases of most mountains. In **temperate climates,** most of these trees are **deciduous.** Many other kinds of plants, such as wildflowers, ferns, and mosses grow in these forests.

In **tropical** climates, it is warm all year. Broad-leaved trees do not lose all their leaves at one time. Other plants, such as vines, orchids, and ferns grow in these forests.

The leaves of many deciduous trees, like these at the base of the Alps Mountains, change color in autumn. Then the leaves fall off the trees.

As it get colder and windier at high **altitudes,** trees have a harder time growing.

Plants at middle altitudes

Farther up the mountains, **coniferous** forests grow. Trees such as pine, fir, and spruce are **conifers.** They make seeds in cones and most have needlelike leaves. Most conifers are **evergreens.** They keep their leaves all year. Ferns, mosses, and wildflowers also grow in the coniferous forests. In the Alps, coniferous forests start at about 4,500 feet (1,370 meters). These forests stop growing at about 5,500 feet (1,675 meters).

The krummholz

If a mountain is tall enough, trees get smaller and farther apart near the top edge of the coniferous forest. The top edge is the krummholz, which means "crooked wood." Here you find clusters of dwarf trees that have been twisted by the strong, cold mountain winds.

11

Trumpet gentians grow in the alpine tundra in the Alps and Pyrenees of Europe. Other **species** of gentians grow on mountains in other parts of the world.

Plants at high altitudes

If a mountain is tall enough, it has a tree line. Above the tree line it is too cold and windy for trees to grow. In this area, **alpine tundra** plants grow. Alpine plants include grasses, mosses, and wildflowers. Lichens also grow here. But they are not plants. A lichen is a **fungus** and an **alga** that live together. Both gain from this living arrangement, which is called **mutualism.**

The snow line

Above a certain level, called the snow line, it is too cold for any plants to grow. Mountains in **tropical** regions that are taller than 15,000 feet (4,500 meters) have snow-capped peaks with no plants. Farther away from the **equator,** the snow line is lower. In the Alps, the snow line is about 9,000 feet (2,700 meters) high.

Plants also change with latitude

Plants that grow on mountains also change with **latitude.** This is the distance north or south of the equator. Many mountains of the Andes are located near the equator. Tropical plants such as palms and mahogany trees grow near the base of these mountains. Vines and orchids also grow in these tropical rain forests. In cold **climates** farther from the equator, such as in the Canadian Rockies, **coniferous** forests grow near the base of the mountains.

The farther north or south of the equator a mountain is, the lower the treeless alpine tundra begins. In warm tropical regions, trees can grow up to the 13,000-foot level (about 4,000 meters). But in the Alps, trees cannot grow above 5,500 feet (1,675 meters).

Tropical rain forest plants like these orchids grow at the bases of many mountains that are near the equator. Rain forests grow where rain falls throughout the year so the plants are never short of water.

4 What Animals Live in the Mountains?

Many different kinds of animals can live near the bases of mountains. But fewer animals can live high in the mountains.

Insects and spiders

Insects such as stoneflies and mayflies live in mountain streams. Beetles, grasshoppers, and butterflies live as high as the **alpine tundra.** Springtails and alpine wetas are small insects that live in cracks in the rocks above the snow line.

Spiders, both large and small, live in different life zones on mountains. Jumping spiders live high on Mount Everest in the Himalayas. They feed on flies and springtails.

Amphibians and reptiles

Few **amphibians** and **reptiles** can live in the cold temperatures high in mountains. These cold-blooded animals have body temperatures that change with their surroundings. Fire salamanders live in the mountains of Europe, Asia, and Africa. Giant salamanders live in the mountains of Japan. Short-horned lizards live in high mountain forests of western North America. Timber rattlesnakes live in the wooded Appalachians.

Japanese giant salamanders can be as long as 5 feet (1 1/2 meters).

Mountain bluebirds spend summers above 5,000 feet (1,525 meters) in the mountains of western North America. They feed on insects.

Birds

Many birds, such as hummingbirds and flycatchers, live near the bottoms of mountains. There they find plenty of seeds, fruits, flowers, and insects for food. American dippers live along clear, rushing mountain streams in North America. They will wade or even swim underwater to find food.

Steller's jays live high in **coniferous** forests of the Rocky Mountains. They feed on insects, berries, and seeds. Golden eagles live in high mountains in North America, Europe, and Asia. They glide above the land searching for small animals and birds. Andean condors soar over the Andes Mountains. They have one of the largest wingspans of any flying bird. Their wingspan is about 10 feet (3 meters). They can live as long as 72 years.

A snow leopard has broad, furry feet that help keep it from sinking into the snow on the high mountain slopes where it lives. It uses its long tail for balance when it leaps between rocks.

Mammals

Mammals of all sizes live in the mountains. Snow leopards live high in the Himalaya Mountains. They feed mainly on wild sheep and goats. Mountain lions live throughout mountains of North and South America. They feed mainly on deer.

Vicuñas are related to camels but they don't have humps. They live only in a few areas high in the Andes of South America. Small family groups feed on grasses and small plants. A male guards each herd. He whistles to warn of danger.

Heather voles are small mammals that live high in the mountains of North America. They live and nest on heather and grasses growing on the floor of **coniferous** forests.

How Do Animals Live in Mountains?

5

Some animals live in the same **life zone** of a mountain all the time. Others move up or down the mountain or leave in winter to find food.

Some animals move in winter

Deer and elk spend summers grazing in **alpine** meadows. They move down to valleys and forests to feed in winter. Black-necked cranes from Tibet are birds that move down the mountains in winter. Other birds **migrate** to mountains in summer but leave in winter. Dusky flycatchers nest in the Rocky Mountains. In winter they migrate to Mexico.

Some animals sleep through winter

Some mountain animals, such as ground squirrels, **hibernate** through cold winters. A hibernating animal goes into a deep sleep. To get ready for winter, it eats large amounts of food. It uses stored body fat as food. A **burrow** protects it from the cold.

Black-necked cranes nest in high-**altitude** marshes. They feed on such things as plant roots, snails, and small fish.

17

Some animals have heavy coats

Yaks, snow leopards, and vicuñas have thick coats that protect them during the cold winters. The fur grows in two layers. A soft, thick undercoat keeps an animal's body from losing heat. Long, slick outer hairs shed snow and keep out wind.

Some animals live in burrows or under rocks

Marmots are large relatives of ground squirrels. They live in family groups in **burrows.** Burrows give them a safe place to have young and to spend the cold winter. Pikas are small mammals related to rabbits. Groups of pikas live among rocks. If one spots an enemy, such as an eagle, it calls out a warning. Then they all dash into cracks in the rocks to hide.

Some animals store food

In mid-summer, pikas start piling up plants in rock shelters. The plants are their winter food. During winter, they travel in tunnels they dig under the snow.

A yak's long, shaggy hair reaches almost to the ground. In spring, it sheds its woolly undercoat.

What's for Dinner in the Mountains?

6

All living things need food. Some living things, like plants, can make their own food. But animals need to find and eat food to live.

Plants

Plants make, or produce, their own food. So they are called **producers.** To make food, plants use carbon dioxide gas from the air and water from the ground. Plants use energy from sunlight to change the carbon dioxide and water into sugars. This process of making food is called **photosynthesis. Broad-leaved** trees, **coniferous** trees, grasses, mosses, ferns, and wildflowers are all mountain producers.

Giant lobelias are producers that grow high in the mountains of Africa. These plants grow for about 20 years, then flower once, and die.

? Did you know?

Algae belong to a group of living things called **protists.** In lichens, the algae are producers. They make food for themselves and the **fungi** they live with.

19

Animals

Animals are called **consumers** because they eat, or consume, food. Some mountain animals, such as yaks, wild sheep, and pikas, eat only plants. These animals are called **herbivores.** Other animals, such as red pandas, ground squirrels, and snow finches, eat both plants and animals. They are **omnivores.** Still others, such as golden eagles, lynxes, and snow leopards, eat only animals. They are **carnivores.**

Mountain goats are herbivores. They feed on mosses and other vegetation found above the tree line in the Rocky Mountains. Rough pads on the bottom of their hooves help them grip the steep ground.

The clean-up crew

Decomposers feed on dead plants and animals and their wastes. **Bacteria, molds,** and some beetles are decomposers. Decomposers break down **nutrients** stored in dead plants and animals. They put them back into the soil, air, and water. Plants use the nutrients to help them grow.

7

How Do Mountain Animals Get Food?

Some mountain animals hunt for food. Others **forage** or **scavenge** for food.

Hunting

Animals that hunt and kill other animals for food are **predators.** Golden eagles are predators. The hunt and eat small **mammals,** snakes, and other birds. Lynxes chase down and eat hares and ground squirrels. So they are predators. Ground squirrels eat plants. But they also hunt and eat insects. So sometimes they are predators. Animals that predators eat are called **prey.** Hares are prey of lynxes and golden eagles. Insects are prey of ground squirrels.

Golden eagles are swift predators. They can snatch a bird out of the air or lift a running rabbit off the ground in an instant.

Some mountain animals are both predators and prey. Mountain chickadees are small birds that eat insects and caterpillars. So, they are predators. However, chickadees are also eaten by golden eagles and owls. So, they are also prey.

Other scavengers often feed on the bodies of dead animals before the bearded vulture eats. It is often left with just the bones.

Foraging

Some animals, such as elk, mountain goats, yaks, vicuñas, and giant pandas, are **foragers.** They move about from place to place, sometimes in groups, to search for food. They search for grasses, buds, leaves, twigs, and lichens to eat.

Scavenging

Some mountain animals are **scavengers.** Scavengers are animals that eat the bodies of animals or plants that are already dead. Andean condors and bearded vultures are scavengers.

Bearded vultures carry bones from dead animals high into the air and drop the bones onto the rocks below. When the bones break open, they can eat the soft marrow inside.

? **Did you know?**

There are fewer than a thousand giant pandas left in the mountains of China.

Planning the menu

The path that shows who eats what is a **food chain.** All living things are parts of food chains. In the **alpine tundra** of mountains in Europe, mountain hares eat alpine grasses and flowers. Golden eagles eat hares.

Another alpine tundra food chain includes snowy voles that eat grasses. The voles are eaten by lynxes. A third food chain includes ibexes that also eat grasses. Young ibexes are eaten by golden eagles. Vultures, who are scavengers, feed on all the animals in the **habitat** that die. All the food chains that are connected in a habitat make up a **food web.** Many living things in a food web are part of more than one food chain.

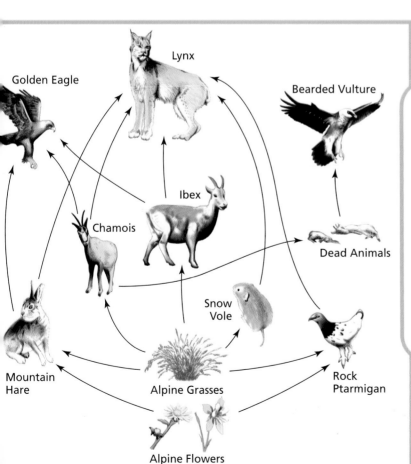

Golden Eagle

Lynx

Bearded Vulture

Ibex

Chamois

Dead Animals

Snow Vole

Mountain Hare

Alpine Grasses

Rock Ptarmigan

Alpine Flowers

In a food web, an arrow is drawn from "dinner" and points to the "diner." So, producers are on the bottom of the web. "Top" predators, animals that no one else eats, are at the top.

23

8 How Do Mountains Affect People?

Mountains can be difficult and dangerous places for people to live. And they can even affect people who don't live in them.

Mountains collect water

Tall mountains store water on their snowy peaks. Melting snow forms rivers that flow into the valleys below. The rivers give people water for drinking, cleaning, and growing crops.

Mountains have landslides and avalanches

Mountains sometimes change in only a few minutes. Heavy rain or a small earthquake can cause a **landslide.** Rocks and soil suddenly crash down the mountainside. A big landslide destroys everything in its path. Large blocks of snow also can break loose. Then, an **avalanche** comes roaring down the mountain. An avalanche can travel as fast as 200 miles (322 kilometers) an hour.

Pine forests high on mountains can often hold back avalanches. In places where the mountain slopes aren't covered by forests, avalanches can destroy whole towns.

Walls of mud 130 feet (40 meters) high swept down valleys below the Nevado del Ruiz volcano, destroying towns.

Volcanic mountains erupt

Living near volcanic mountains can be dangerous. In 1902, Mount Pelée on the Caribbean island of Martinique erupted. Hot gases and ash raced down the mountain. A town at its base was destroyed. More than 30,000 people were killed.

On November 13, 1985, Colombia's Nevado del Ruiz volcano erupted. Heat from the volcano melted snow on the mountain. Melted snow mixed with soil and formed huge mudflows. Nearly 23,000 people died.

Living at high altitudes

High in mountains, the air is thinner and there is not as much oxygen in it. Native people who live high in the Andes are **adapted** to the thin air. They have larger lungs that allow them to take in more air with each breath. Their blood has more red blood cells to carry oxygen to all parts of their bodies.

25

9 How Do People Affect Mountains?

Few people live in mountains. But many people use mountains and their **resources.**

The kakapo of New Zealand is the world's only flightless, **nocturnal** parrot. Fewer than 100 of these birds are left.

People damage habitats

In many places, mountain forests have been cut down. Animals have lost food and shelter. Without tree roots to hold soil in place, the soil washes away. Flooding, avalanches, and landslides happen more often.

People also mine **minerals** in mountains. **Pollution** from mining harms water and land.

When New Zealand was settled, people brought in **predators,** such as pet cats. These predators have caused some flightless mountain birds to become **extinct** or **endangered.**

People hunt animals

Many mountain animals are endangered and are protected by laws. Rangers try to protect them. But **poachers** sometimes kill them anyway. Snow leopards are killed for their fur. Mountain gorillas live in mountains of Rwanda and Uganda in Africa. Poachers sell their body parts.

The Appalachian National Scenic Trail passes through 14 states, two national parks, and eight national forests. It follows the crests of mountains from Mt. Katahdin in Maine to Springer Mountain in Georgia.

People use mountains for recreation

People hike in mountains like the Appalachians. They also climb high mountains like the Himalayas. Mountain climbers leave trash in Himalayas because it takes too much energy to bring it back down the mountain. Some people climb up just to collect the trash. People also build ski resorts in mountains. Ski resorts can destroy mountain **habitats.**

People protect mountains

Many parks and nature reserves have been created to protect mountain habitats. Swiss National Park protects animals like chamois and ibexes. It also protects edelweiss plants. Other parks in the Alps protect golden eagles. Fiordland National Park in New Zealand protects many species of mountain plants and animals. Mountains are beautiful places. People must protect them and use them carefully.

27

Fact File

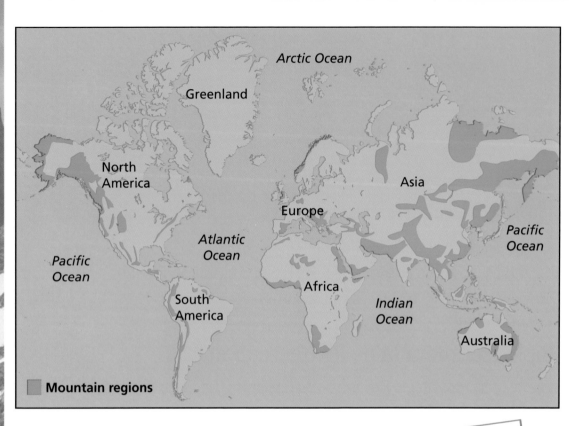

Mountain regions

Year of the Mountain
The year 2002 was declared the International Year of the Mountain by the United Nations. Programs were established to "improve the lives of mountain people, protect fragile mountain ecosystems, and promote peace and stability in mountain regions."

About 770 million people live in mountain regions. About 50 million people visit mountains each year. In the Alps, the Andes, the Himalayas, and the Rockie Mountains, as much as 90 percent of the local people's income is from mountain tourism.

Earth's Mountains

Mountain	Location	Facts
Alaska Range	south central Alaska	Mount McKinley, also called Denali, (20,320 ft*/ 6,194 m**) is the highest point in North America.
Alps	central Europe	The youngest of Earth's great mountain ranges; Mont Blanc (14,771 ft/4,807 m) is the tallest peak; the Alps in France, Austria, Switzerland, and Italy have the most deadly avalanches every year.
Altai Mountains	Western Mongolia and Kazakstan in Asia	Contain rich deposits of lead, zinc, gold, silver, copper, and iron; Belukha (14,783 ft/4,506 m) is the tallest peak.
Andes	western South America	The longest mountain range on Earth—stretching 4,500 miles (7,200 km); Aconcagua (22,840 ft/6,960 m) is the tallest peak.
Appalachians	eastern United States	The oldest mountains in North America; Mount Mitchell (6,684 ft/2,037 m) is the tallest peak.
Atlas Mountains	northwestern Africa	Jebel Toubkal (13,665 ft/4,165 m) is the tallest peak.
Cascade Range	along the coast of Washington, Oregon and northern California	Contains many snowcapped volcanic mountains, including Mount St. Helens; Mount Rainier (14,410 ft/ 4,392 m) is the tallest peak.
Drakensberg Mountains	South Africa	Injasuti (11,181 ft/3,408 m) is the tallest peak.
Great Dividing Range/ Australian Alps	eastern Australia	Mount Kosciusko (7,310 ft/2,228 m) is the tallest peak; it and other tall peaks are snow covered in winter.
Himalayas	Asia, beginning at the northern edge of India.	The highest mountain range on Earth; Mount Everest (29,108 ft/8,872 m) is the world's highest mountain.
Pyrenees	between France and Spain	Pico de Aneto (11,168 ft/3,404 m), in Spain, is the tallest peak.
Rocky Mountains	western North America (United States and Canada)	Mount Elbert (14,432 ft/4,399 m) in Colorado is the tallest peak; in the United States, Colorado, Alaska, and Utah have the most deadly avalanches.
Southern Alps	South Island, New Zealand	Mount Cook (12,349 ft/3,764 m) is the tallest peak.
Ural Mountains	between Europe and Asia	Toward the Arctic the mountains are covered with tundra plants; farther south some conifers grow; Mount Narodnaya (6,214 ft/1,894 m) is the tallest peak.

*ft = feet
**m =meters

Glossary

adapted changed to live under certain conditions

alga (plural: algae) a producer that lives in damp places

alpine living on mountains above the tree line

altitude how high a place is above the ocean or sea level

amphibian animal with a moist skin that lives on land but lays its eggs in water. Frogs, toads, and salamanders are amphibians.

avalanche large mass of snow and ice loosened from a mountainside that swiftly moves down the mountain

bacteria living things too small to be seen except with a microscope. Some bacteria are decomposers.

biodiversity variety of life, or number of different species, in a habitat

broad-leaved having wide, flat leaves

burrow hole dug in the ground by animals for shelter

carnivore animal that eats only other animals

climate average weather conditions in an area over a long period of time

conifer trees that make their seeds in cones

coniferous making seeds in cones

consumer living thing that needs plants for food

deciduous shedding leaves at a particular season

decomposer consumer that puts nutrients from dead plants and animals back into the soil, air, and water.

endangered likely to become extinct. Kakapos and snow leopards are endangered animals.

equator imaginary circle around Earth halfway between the North Pole and the South Pole

erosion moving of soil and rocks by water, wind or ice

evergreen having green leaves or needles all year long

extinct no longer existing on Earth

food chain path that shows who eats what in a habitat

food web group of connected food chains in a habitat

forage wander about in search of food

forager animal or person that wanders about searching for food

fungus (plural: fungi) living thing that feeds on dead or living plant or animal matter. Mushrooms and molds are fungi.

habitat place where a plant or animal naturally lives

herbivore animal that eats only plants

hibernate spend the winter in a state in which an animal's breathing, heart rate, and body temperature is greatly reduced

landslide mass of rock and soil sliding down a steep slope

latitude distance north or south of the equator

life zone habitat found at a particular altitude or a mountain

mammal warm-blooded animal that breathes with lungs, has a bony skeleton, has hair or fur, and produces milk to feed its young

migrate move from one place to another with the change of seasons

mineral any material dug from the earth by mining. Gold, iron, and diamonds are minerals.

mold living thing that uses dead plants and animals for food. Molds are decomposers.

mutualism relationship between two species that helps both living things

nocturnal active at night

nutrient material that is needed for the growth of a plant or animal

omnivore animal that eats plants and animals

photosynthesis process by which green plants trap the sun's energy and use it to change carbon dioxide and water into sugars

poacher person who kills animals that are protected by law

pollution harmful materials in the water, air, or land

predator animal that hunts and eats other animals

prey animal that is hunted and eaten by other animals

producer living thing that can use sunlight to make its own food

protist type of living thing that is neither a plant nor an animal. Algae are protists.

range group of mountains

reptile land animal with a scaly skin. Snakes, lizards, turtles, and crocodiles are reptiles.

resource anything that meets a need that people, plants, or animals have

scavenge feed on the bodies of dead animals

scavenger animal that eats the bodies of animals that are already dead

species group of living things that are enough alike that they can mate and reproduce

temperate has warm or hot summers and cool or cold winters

tropical region near the equator that is warm to hot all year round

tundra cold, treeless area

More Books to Read

Bograd, Larry. *The Rocky Mountains.* New York: Benchmark Books, 2000.

Fowler, Allan. *Living in the Mountains.* Danbury, Conn.: Children's Press, 2000.

Gray, Susan Heinrichs. *Mountains.* Mankato, Minn.: Compass Point Books, 2000.

Green, Jen. *People of the Mountains.* Austin, Tex.: Raintree Steck-Vaughn, 1998.

Index

adaptation 6, 18, 25
algae 19
alpine tundra region 14, 23
alpine tundra plants 12, 13
Alps 4, 7, 9, 12
altitude 4
amphibians 14
Andes Mountains 4, 7, 8, 9, 13, 15
animals 6, 7, 14–18, 20–23, 26
Appalachian Mountains 5, 14, 27
avalanches 24

Bear Mountain 4
Bern, Switzerland 7
biodiversity 9
birds 15, 17
borders 7
broad-leaved trees 10, 19
burrows 17, 18

carnivores 20
Cascade Mountains 8
cities 7, 9
climate 6, 8, 10, 13
condors 15
coniferous trees 11, 13, 15, 16, 19
consumers 20

deciduous trees 10
decomposers 20
Denver, Colorado 7
dippers 15

eagles 15, 20
equator 13
erosion 5
evergreen trees 11

Fiordland National Park 27
food chain 23
food web 23
foragers 22
formation 4

giant pandas 22
gold mining 9

heather voles 16
herbivores 20
hibernating animals 17
Himalaya Mountains 4, 5, 7, 14, 16, 27

Indian cultures 7
insects 14
iron mining 9

krummholz 11

La Paz, Bolivia 7
landslides 24
latitude 13
lichens 12, 22
life zones 6, 9, 17
lizards 14

mammals 16, 21
marmots 18
migrating birds 17
minerals 9, 26
mining 9, 26
Mount Everest 4, 14
Mount Pelée 25
Mount St. Helens 5
mountain lions 16
mudflows 25
mutualism 12

natural resources 9, 26
Nevado del Ruiz volcano 25
nutrients 20

omnivores 20

Paricutin volcano 5
people 7, 24–27
photosynthesis 19
pikas 18, 20

plants 6, 7, 10–13, 19, 20
poachers 26
pollution 26
predators 21, 26
prey 21
producers 19
protists 19
Pyrenees Mountains 7

Quito, Ecuador 7

rain shadow effect 8
ranges 4
rattlesnakes 14
reptiles 14
Rocky Mountains 4, 7, 9, 13, 15

salamanders 14
salt mining 9
Salzburg, Austria 9
scavengers 22
silver mining 9
snow leopards 16
snow line 12
spiders 14
Steller's jays 15
Swiss National Park 27

temperate climates 10
tin mining 9
tree line 12
tropical climates 10, 12

undercoats 18
Ural Mountains 5, 7, 9

vicuñas 16, 18
volcanic mountains 4, 5, 25

zinc mining 9